Insider Secrets to Financing Your Real Estate Investments

Insider Secrets to Financing Your Real Estate Investments

What Every Real Estate Investor Needs to Know about Finding and Financing Your Next Deal

Frank Gallinelli

McGraw-Hill

New York   Chicago   San Francisco   Lisbon
London   Madrid   Mexico City   Milan   New Delhi
San Juan   Seoul   Singapore   Sydney   Toronto

3 4 5 6 7 8 9 0   DSH/DSH   0 1 0 9

ISBN 0-07-144543-9

This publication is designed to provide accurate and authoritative information in regard to the subject matter covered. It is sold with the understanding that neither the author nor the publisher is engaged in rendering legal, accounting, or other professional service. If legal advice or other expert assistance is required, the services of a competent professional person should be sought.
> —*From a Declaration of Principles jointly adopted by Committee of the American Bar Association and a Committee of Publishers.*

McGraw-Hill books are available at special quantity discounts to use as premiums and sales promotions, or for use in corporate training programs. For more information, please write to the Director of Special Sales, McGraw-Hill Professional, Two Penn Plaza, New York, NY 10121-2298. Or contact your local bookstore.

This book is printed on recycled, acid-free paper containing a minimum of 50% recycled, de-inked fiber.

Library of Congress Cataloging-in-Publication Data

Gallinelli, Frank.
  Insider secrets to financing your real estate investments : what every real estate investor needs to know about finding & financing your next deal / by Frank Gallinelli.
    p.   cm.
  Includes index.
  ISBN 0-07-144543-9 (pbk. : alk. paper)
  1. Real estate investment.   2. Real estate investment—Finance.   I. Title.
  HD1382.5.G348   2005
  332.63'24—dc22

                                                            2004023701

For Keith and Nicole.

No success in life could be as important to me as you are.
I grow more proud of you every day.

Contents

PART III
THE OFFER, THE CLOSING, AND THEN WHAT?

Acknowledgments

However much I would like to imagine that I know everything about my topic, there are moments when I stare at a blank manuscript page and it just sits there laughing at me. Those were the moments when I sent out pleas for help and I want to thank the friends and colleagues who came to my aid:

Michael P. Buckley, Director, M.S. in Real Estate Development Program at Columbia University, a veritable font of wisdom on all matters of real estate investment, development, and finance, who tolerates and even encourages my guest lectures at the University; Ken Ferrari, managing partner of Marketplace Mortgage of Plainville, Connecticut, someone who knows and cares about his profession and who helped me understand residential lending from the his side of the desk; attorneys Andy Garson and David Slepian of Fairfield, Connecticut, who always listen patiently to my convoluted deals and who set me straight when I purported to explain the fine point of closings and real estate titles; Suzanne Kliegerman, Senior Vice President, Real Estate Lending Division, Commerce Bank, New York who helped me see real estate finance through the eyes of a portfolio lender; Bill Wilson, Jr., CPA with Van Brunt, Du Biago of Stamford, Connecticut, who helps keep my books (and sometimes me) in balance.

I also want to thank several thousands of the customers of my software company, RealData. Over the past 23 years you've shared many vivid accounts of your real estate investment and development deals—your plans, your successes, your problems, your creative solutions. That interaction has allowed me to participate vicariously in many more deals than any one person could reasonably expect to experience in one career. You're the best.

Introduction

"There's a first time for everything." No doubt you've heard this threadbare cliché more than once in your life. We're all adults here, so it's safe to tell you: It's true.

Among the experiences you apparently aspire to undergo for the first time (or possibly just the second or third) is to invest in real estate. That's why you're reading this book instead of doing something you might enjoy. I'm bringing this subject up on the very first page so that you can line up your expectations. For whom is this book written? What's in it for you?

First of all, you are not a dummy. On the contrary, I suspect you're quite bright and would like to apply that intelligence to a field where you can build some significant wealth. You may not expect (or even want) to get private-jet rich, but you at least want to build the kind of assets that can put your kids through college, fund your retirement, and perhaps even exempt you from the nine to five routine earlier than you had originally planned.

These are realistic goals, but to achieve them you need to take the first steps, which brings us back to the "first time for everything" chestnut. In whatever you now do for a living, you do it well because you first learned the basics and then built up experience. Real estate investing is no different. You need to start with the basics, not with exotic or obscure get-rich-quick techniques. Then you need to implement those fundamentals and develop your skills through practice.

Depending on your professional and business and life experience, some of the material in this book might be obvious to you, while other content will be entirely new and unfamiliar. Perhaps you're not really a first-timer but have already purchased one or even a few investment properties. Is there anything here for you? There is a lot to learn about real estate invest-ing—certainly more than can be covered in any one book —so yes, there will be some lessons in this volume for you as well. Before your habits become entrenched, see how they compare to the methods I discuss here. You want to develop a best-practices approach to investing.

I intend this book to serve as "Real Estate Investing 101." I believe it makes an excellent place for you to start your investment career because it provides you with an overview of the process: where to find candidate properties; how to choose one; where and how to get financing; how to negotiate and close the deal; and how to get off on the right foot once you're an owner. It also adds a healthy dose of tips that you might otherwise need to learn through trial and error. I've been a real estate investor for more than 30 years; learn from my mistakes so you can make new ones of your own.

At several places in this text I'll refer to another book of mine, *What Every Real Estate Investor Needs to Know About Cash Flow*, also published by McGraw-Hill. The financial analysis of an income property is an essen-tial part of the process of choosing a worthwhile and promising investment. Because this volume serves as an overview, I cover just the high points of financial analysis here. If you decide that you want to develop a more com-plete understanding of this topic, I suggest you take a look at the *Cash Flow* book.

As in my previous book, you'll find that this one is liberally garnished with "Rules of Thumb." These little snippets of advice represent more opin-ion (mine) than fact. They may not fit every place and time, so be sure to measure them against the realities of your situation.

You will also find that I provide resources online that you can use in conjunction with this book. To access them, go to realdata.com/secrets.

Now it's time to start. What better place than at the beginning? Before you can become a successful real estate investor, you need to find some properties. And before you do *that*, you need to find your comfort zone. Let's start.

Insider Secrets to Financing Your Real Estate Investments

PART 1

HOW TO CHOOSE A REAL ESTATE INVESTMENT

1

Identify Your Comfort Zone

There is an old saying—if you don't know where you're going, any road will get you there. Succeeding as a real estate investor, or as anything else for that matter, requires that you develop a plan and then follow it. The very fact that you want to succeed as an "investor" establishes that your main purpose is not to flip properties for a quick profit but rather to select investments that will provide a meaningful return—and gain—over time.

Part of your plan should be to establish basic guidelines concerning properties you'll try to acquire. Be proactive rather than reactive—define what you're looking for; don't just respond to whatever crosses your field of vision. Especially if you are working toward your first real estate investment, you want to seek out a property whose cost, location, and type will fit best with your financial resources, skills, and experience. The first step then in finding a suitable investment property is finding your comfort zone.

1. **Identify a price range**

   How much cash do you have available to you? How much financing are you likely to obtain? (We'll talk about this topic in greater detail in a later section.) If banks are offering loans at 80 percent of a property's value and you have $50,000 to work with, then $250,000 would repre-

sent a reasonable purchase price. You might choose to look at properties with asking prices approaching $300,000.

Keep in mind that, depending on the type of property and its condition, you might be wise to hold back some cash as a reserve to deal
with unanticipated repairs or with a loss of rent income.

2. Choose a location

You will certainly read somewhere about the virtues of scouring the
country looking for great investment deals. As the argument goes, if
you make a spectacular deal you'll be able to afford the services of a
local management company to run the property. Actually, there is a lot
of truth to that argument but there is also an important caveat. If you
are a relative novice at real estate investing, this is not a prudent way to
start. If you have never tried to manage a property yourself, then it's
very difficult for you to have a sound, long-distance sense of how matters are going. Is the local employment market or business climate
changing? Is the rental market changing? Is the management company
doing an acceptable job? Is the property being kept clean and in good
repair? With experience, you learn to stay attuned to these issues.
However, if you start off owning properties you seldom or never see,
occupied and managed by people you seldom or never see, then you
miss the opportunity to develop that kind of experience.

If starting off with properties in a remote location is a bad idea,
then starting off with properties nearby must a good idea. Distance is
one consideration, but not the only one. Yes, the property should be
close enough so you can get in your car and go there without having to
pack a bag. Equally important, as the anvil salesman in *Music Man*
says, "You gotta know the territory." When you purchase an income
property, it can be very valuable to understand the neighborhood
dynamics and demographics. If you are looking at property in a residential area, is it characterized primarily by owner-occupants, tenants,
or a mix? Is there very little turnover among rental units or is it an area
favored by students, with frequent turnover? What is the typical rental
rate? If the property is commercial—say, retail—are stores doing well?
Are there vacancies? Is parking adequate? Do businesses seem to come
and go? Is there an apparent "dead spot?" (Just about everyone has seen
a place where a dozen restaurants have tried and failed.)

These are some but not all of the questions you want to answer about a neighborhood. The more of an expert you become in the dynamics of a given area, the more success you are likely to achieve, both in selecting and in managing income properties. In short, the more you know about the territory, the more comfort you'll find in your comfort zone.

Sometimes, buying property locally is just not an option. During a recent lecture tour I spoke with quite a number of people who said, "Real estate prices have risen so dramatically here that it simply isn't possible to purchase anything that can even support its own financing. We have no choice but to look outside the immediate area."

If you *must* buy outside your area—far enough outside that you cannot visit regularly—then you need to have an alter ego or two that you trust implicitly. Essentially, this is similar to my "know the territory" advice except now you'll have to rely on other knowledgeable individuals to be your eyes and ears. You will need a good local broker who will take the time to make sure you understand the dynamics of the area; and you will need a reliable property manager to rent the property and handle landlord-tenant issues. For long-distance investing to work, you have to feel confident that the broker and manager are capable and honest beyond reproach.

3. **Select a type of property**

   You certainly don't have to purchase the same kind of property every time, but if this is your first purchase then you should consider how a particular type of property might suit your personality and skills. If you have experience in business, you might feel right at home with commercial property. If you're comfortable dealing with people, perhaps you'll start with a small, multifamily property. If you're good at delegating responsibility and measuring performance, you might do best with a larger apartment building where you use a property manager.

   Let's look at some of the most common choices along with their pros and cons:

   a. *Single-family residence or condominium*
      Pros:
      i. Among the easiest types of property to manage because there is just one tenant.

  ii.   They are abundant; you have plenty to choose from.

 iii.   If you already own your own single-family home, then there should be nothing about the physical property that is unfamiliar to you.

 iv.   You can negotiate a lease where the tenant is responsible for all utilities, yard care, snow removal, even property taxes. Obviously, the more extras the tenant must pay, the lower the base rent he or she will expect to pay. The difference might still be worthwhile to you as the landlord because passing these expenses through reduces your uncertainty as to operating costs and reduces your management responsibilities.

  v.   At some point you might choose to move into the property yourself. Under the current tax code, living there for two years could earn you a significant capital gains tax break (as in, "no tax").

Cons:

  i.   Single-family residences might be more difficult to rent than apartments because the rental rates are typically higher (see ii. below).

 ii.   Single-family residences typically are valued not by their ability to produce income but rather by market data—that is, sales of comparable homes in the area. Even though you might charge rent that seems high compared to that of an apartment, the maximum rent you can achieve may still not be enough to cover your mortgage payments and expenses. You might only realize a positive cash flow after several years of ownership and only realize a meaningful profit from the eventual resale. To estimate whether you are likely to cover your costs with a single-family investment property, you will definitely need to develop cash flow projections. You would be wise to make such projections with all of your potential income-property investments and you'll see how to do so in a later section.

b. *Multifamily property (two to four units)*
Pros:

  i.   Not as abundant as single-families but still plenty to choose from.

ii. There is a fair chance that you have lived in a property like this at some point in your life so the environment is not unfamiliar.

iii. Generally easy to rent.

iv. May have separate metering of all utilities and heat. Be wary of those that do not.

v. You could choose to live in one of the units right from the outset. Under current tax rules your owner-occupied unit would be a personal residence that you could not depreciate but which you might be able to exempt from most or all capital gains tax; the rented units would be your investment property, with depreciation allowed for tax purposes. If you are an owner-occupant you might also be able to obtain more favorable mortgage and insurance rates.

Cons:

i. Multifamily homes tend to be older, so you may encounter higher repair and maintenance costs.

c. *Multifamily property (greater than four units)*

Pros:

i. Usually can produce a strong cash flow.

ii. Safety in numbers; if a tenant moves out unexpectedly in a two-family house, half of your revenue stream dries up. One tenant in a 30-unit building is a small blip on the radar.

iii. Generally easy to rent.

iv. Opportunity for additional income from laundry facilities, parking, etc.

Cons:

i. Leasing and oversight can be a full-time job; may require a property management company.

ii. May not have separate metering of all utilities and heat.

iii. May experience high wear and tear on common areas by virtue of the number of people using them.

d. *Office Building*

Pros:

i. They come in sizes to fit every budget, from a converted frame house with a doctor and dentist to a high-rise with corporate tenants.

ii. Possibility of long-term tenancies; if so, then the income stream can be stable and re-leasing activity minimal.

iii. Opportunity for additional income from pooled reception and secretarial services, high-speed Internet access, parking, vending, etc.

Cons:

i.   Know your market: Historically there have been plenty of instances of overbuilding in the office sector. When this occurs, there can be high vacancy rates as well as downward pressure on rents that lasts for years.

ii. If you have never been a commercial office tenant, then you need to get up to speed on the provisions that are common to such leases. You'll be dealing with issues not normally addressed in residential leases.

e. *Retail (small, freestanding through strip center)*
    Pros:

i.   Like offices, they can range in size and cost from a neighborhood convenience store to a strip center with 10 or more stores. (I will not discuss larger shopping centers here; if you get to that level, you will have outgrown this book.)

ii. Also like offices, they offer the possibility of long-term tenancies.

Cons:

i.   Again, know your market: The property will do well only if the retail businesses thrive. Location is important with all real estate, but you will live or die by the location of retail property.

ii. You may need to learn about issues that are unique to retail centers, such as "tenant mix," i.e., filling the center with businesses that complement each other but do not compete. (For example, a convenience store and a dry cleaner can contribute to a good mix. "Honey, when you pick up your shirts would you also stop for some bread and milk?"

iii. If you have never been a retail tenant, then you also need to learn about the specialized provisions in retail leases.

f. *Industrial*
    Pros:
    i.   There are many kinds of property that might fall under the gen-
         eral heading "industrial." Don't try going after the General
         Motors plant as your first venture. There are enough smaller,
         local properties that you can consider.
    ii. Among smaller industrial properties, many are single-tenant—
         for example, a machine shop, repair facility, parts fabricator,
         cabinet maker. A somewhat larger building will perhaps have
         just a few tenants leasing warehouse space. The fewer the num-
         ber of tenants, usually the less intensive your management
         activity will be.
    iii. Self-storage facilities (commonly built in industrial zones)
         have traditionally provided high returns; you might also find
         attractive financing terms.
    Cons:
    i.   Depending on the tenant's business, industrial use of a proper-
         ty can lead to environmental contamination. Remediation can
         be tremendously expensive. You can use lease language to let
         the tenant know that you're dead serious about this issue, but
         all the lease contracts in the world won't help if the tenant con-
         taminates the property and goes bankrupt. You need to be both
         visible and vigilant to discourage your tenant from even think-
         ing about improper or careless disposal of any type of toxic
         material.

g. *The Rest—Hotels, Motels, Mobile Home Parks, Raw Land, etc.*
    Neither pros nor cons to discuss here. Except for raw land, I would
    characterize these as business enterprises, not income-property
    investments. Running a motel and operating as a landlord are fun-
    damentally different ways of spending your time. Leasing raw land
    fits the landlord model better, but it's a highly specialized, do-it-
    once-and-you're-done-for-30-years undertaking. In other words, it
    deserves a book of its own.

Rule of Thumb: *Finding your comfort zone is a three-step process:*
1. Set a price range. 2. Identify at least one but not more than a few

geographic areas that are reachable and where you have or can develop a good understanding of the real estate market and the demographics. 3. Choose the type or types of property that suit your skills and personality.

Now you have candidates to choose from. All you have to do is pick one.

2

Where Do You Find Good Properties to Buy?

As you move through this book, you'll learn about comparing alternative investment properties, finding and obtaining financing, closing the deal, and what I hope will be an ample list of other useful topics. Before you can do any that, you need to find some properties to look at. Where might you find them?

If you're considering the purchase of a real estate investment, then there is a good chance that you are already a homeowner and have had some experience shopping for property. All of the usual suspects that apply to home shopping can also provide you with access to income properties that are for sale:

1. Real Estate Agents

A good agent who knows that you're a serious buyer can be a very valuable asset. Later we'll talk about financial leverage, but there is also, of course, the leveraging of your time and effort. If you have a capable individual screening potential choices for you, then you greatly increase your chances of identifying suitable properties. Real estate investing is all about the numbers; if you can select from among 5, 10, or even more potential investments instead of just one or two, your chances of success must necessarily improve.

2. For Sale by Owner Signs

For Sale by Owner signs can also lead you to some worthwhile properties. Most "Fizzbos," as they are called, want to sell their own property in order to save the commission they would otherwise pay to an agent. Because this motivation is not a particularly well-kept secret, you, as the buyer, expect to share in that saving, diluting its presumed benefit right off the bat.

Sellers who have not been counseled by an agent might set an asking price that is inappropriate—often unrealistically high, but sometimes *below* market. Finding just one gem can make it worth the effort to search out FSBO properties.

3. Newspaper Advertisements (from Agents, Owners, Banks)

Your local newspaper is a valuable tool. Obviously it's a source of direct information because agents and private sellers will advertise their properties here. Scouring the small print of the legal notices will also provide you with useful leads. Banks and other mortgage lenders advertise their foreclosure sales in these legal notices. Depending on your location, your chances of finding a good property being sold at foreclosure can range from negligible to good. Even if you check these notices and see nothing that is even remotely appealing, keep checking. It won't take you very long to scan them and, as with the FSBOs, it takes only one great investment to justify the effort.

There are other ways your local newspaper can benefit your budding investment career. Many papers publish information about property sales regularly. This is a not a substitute for careful research at your Town Hall or County Assessor, but it can help to give you a sense of trends and the level of activity in different neighborhoods. Do you notice an increasing number of sales in one section of town, perhaps along with a rise in prices that is greater than in other areas? Even if these are single-family home sales, they can serve as an alert to anticipate greater demand for apartments and commercial space.

Another use for the newspaper (assuming you don't have a parakeet) is to help you find an agent who is likely to fit well with your investment goals. Among the first decisions you will make are, "What kind of property do I want to buy and in what location?" Often you'll find that experienced, successful agents get to be that way because they specialize. They become very knowledgeable about a particular area and sometimes about a particular kind of property in that area. Say that you want to buy small, multifamily properties within a 2-mile radius of your home. Assuming that a reasonable quantity of such properties exists, you should be able to identify a small number of agents who are handling most of that business. It might not be all of ABC Realty Co., whose signs you see in the area, but rather one particular person in that company. As you study the "For Sale" ads over time, you will be able to identify those agents who can help you find the kind of property you want in the area you prefer.

4. Your Own Advertisements

The conventional use of newspapers is to place ads for property that is for sale. Turn that thinking around and place an ad seeking a property to buy. It's quite common that an owner who is just beginning to entertain thoughts of selling or who is merely curious about what's going on in the market will browse the classifieds. You might be contacted by a broker who knows of a property not actively for sale but on which he or she can obtain an "open" listing to represent the property to a particular buyer—you.

Make your ad fairly specific. Mention the location or locations as well as the types of property you would consider. Don't specify a price, although you might want to mention the amount of your planned equity investment if it's substantial. As an alternative to discussing money in the ad, you can indicate the size of the property you're seeking—for example, "Apartment building, 20–300 units" or "Retail strip, 10,000–20,000 square feet."

You're certain to get responses that don't even resemble your requirements, but don't be discouraged. You're looking for just a few pearls.

5. Internet Searches

Finally, there is the Internet. Each year the number of online databases offering information about properties for sale seems to multiply. These services come, go, and merge at an impressive pace. One that I have watched and that survived the dot-bomb shakeout is loopnet.com. They started out in 1995, then merged with another provider in 2001. They give you access to an enormous inventory of property for sale and for lease. Even if you don't find what you're looking for, their database can be a good way to see the kinds of prices and lease rates that prevail in an area and to identify brokers who are handling certain property types in a given area.

I suggest that you use your search engine of choice to find results for terms such as "real estate listing service." Most of these databases try to be national in scope. If you want to focus your attention on a fairly small geographic area, then you have limited chances of finding much inventory in some of the smaller databases. Nonetheless, the searching is easy and the rewards can be great.

There are other ways you might use the Internet to ferret out investment properties. The major Internet portal sites, such as Yahoo and MSN, each have hundreds of discussion forums (called "groups") dedicated to real estate. In most cases you can read the postings that members make even if you don't join the group. If you would like to post a question or comment, or reply to a member, then you need to join the group. A fair number of these groups exist to help buyers find properties and to help sellers find buyers. Even more of the groups serve as question-and-answer forums whose members represent a range from beginner to experienced. While some of the discussions might be banal, you can often find valuable information and get answers from expert members. The best course of action is to visit a few of these forums and identify those where both the topics and the level of discourse suit your needs.

For those who get involved in commercial real estate, I'll mention another Web site: The Dealmakers (www.property.com) bill themselves as the oldest commercial real estate portal on the Internet, and I have been a subscriber to some of their email forums long enough to believe that they probably are. Many of the messages on their forum are property "haves" and "wants," so if you delve into the commercial sector, this can be a valuable resource.

The Real Estate Cyberspace Society (www.recyber.com) is another site you should be aware of. They too were early adopters of the Internet and offer resources to both commercial and residential investors. RECyber's mission goes beyond their discussion forums. They also provide or recommend a variety of resources and offer "gurus" as part of a subscription membership.

Finally, in yet another fit of shameless self-promotion, I must suggest that you take advantage of free materials provided on my own company's site, www.realdata.com. Although our primary business is software for analysis of real estate investments and development, a significant part of realdata.com is devoted to educational content. Our reasoning is transparent: The better you understand investment and development concepts and techniques, the greater benefit you'll derive from our software. At any particular moment you should find a good collection of instructional articles as well as occasional recommendations of third-party resources we think are especially worthwhile.

6. The Not-So-Usual Suspects

Unlike personal residences, most investment properties are for sale even when they're not for sale. If you were to approach the owner of the Dutch colonial around the corner from your home and say, "Hi. Nice tulips. Want to sell your house?" you would probably receive a response that combined disbelief with outright hostility. You wouldn't really expect anyone to throw grandma and the Steinway on the back of a pickup and pull a suburban *Grapes of Wrath* just because you expressed an interest in purchasing their home.

On the other hand, the majority of investment properties are not owner-occupied. There are exceptions, of course, and the most common are multifamily homes where the owner lives in one of the apartments and commercial properties where the owner operates a business from the site. The rest, however, are owned primarily by people who have the same motivation that caused you to read this book: a desire to achieve a return on investment. If they're smart investors, then they don't have an emotional attachment to their property. It's an investment, like 1000 shares of Big Box Retailer.

Even though the owner of an income property is not actively seeking a buyer, he or she is likely to welcome an inquiry. It shouldn't be difficult for you to put yourself in the place of a typical owner: *The property is running well enough and makes relatively few demands on your time and attention. You could benefit from a sale, but right now you have more urgent priorities to deal with. Selling sounds like an effort and distraction—unless someone makes it easy by initiating the process.*

This is not the spin-master exercise it sounds like. There are plenty of reasons why an investment property owner would want to sell. The first and most important reason is intrinsic to the investment process itself. You'll see a number of examples in this book emphasizing that you must look at a real estate investment not so much as a physical property but as an income stream. It is a series of cash flows, and the last of these cash flows is the one you receive when you sell the property. Consider if you will, a comparison—albeit imperfect—to a stock investment. You could benefit from ongoing dividends paid by the stock, but you don't truly realize the fruits of your investment until you sell that stock. Likewise, the sale of a real estate investment is the conclusion you expect and look forward to. It's the last and usually the largest cash flow.

It's not the end of the world, just the end of the deal. The investor bought the property so he or she could resell it someday for a profit. If you choose to approach the owner and express an interest in an otherwise unmarketed property, you're suggesting that today might be that day.

Inevitability it might account for the fact that the owner must sell eventually in order to reach her investment goals, but why sell today? There are ample possibilities and even if they appear mundane, they can be compelling.

1. Perhaps most obvious is the proverbial bird in the hand. It can cost money to find a buyer when the seller wants one, but here you are. No fuss, no bother, no advertising costs, no brochures, no commission.
2. A second reason is that the price is right. It's unlikely that you want to be in the position of offering more than a property is worth, but if your offer is both fair and acceptable to the owner, then that person should be thinking, "Does it make sense to expend the time, effort, and cost to chase after a higher offer? Will I really end up ahead if I do?"

3. The owner might have used up all of the allowable depreciation on the property and thus exhausted its potential for sheltering any of its income from taxes. If that's the case, the timing could be right for the owner to sell this property, buy another, and start the depreciation clock ticking again.

4. Perhaps the cash flow has dried up because of bad management or loss of a key tenant. The current owner would like to get out, but this could be an opportunity for you to take corrective action and create value.

5. The owner might also be ready to retire or to move out of the area, making management of the property inconvenient.

6. He or she might also simply be at a point in life when cash in the present has greater appeal than cash in the future. The teenage triplets are all going off to college next fall; need cash *now*.

You don't know until you ask; if you ask often enough then you'll encounter the kinds of answers that lead you to a deal.

Before you approach any owner, you should run through this brief checklist:

1. Be certain you're familiar with the area.
    a. What attracts people to this neighborhood?
    b. What motivates people to move away?
    c. What is the turnover in rentals and sales?
    d. What is the market for rentals?
2. Drive around and select particular properties that you might really want to own.
    a. If you're looking for a property in pristine condition or a fixer-upper or a neighborhood convenience center, make a list of the properties that fit your objective.
    b. Never pick addresses at random or all the addresses on a street.
3. Do your homework.
    a. Go to the town hall or county assessor and find out who owns the property and for how long. Examine the address to which the tax bill is being sent. If it's different from the property address, then the building is probably not owner-occupied.
    b. Find out what the current and perhaps the previous owner paid.
    c. Go to the tax assessor's office and find the assessed value.

d. Examine the assessor's field card so you'll know as much as you can about the physical property—its square footage, amenities, layout, etc.

4. DO NOT approach the tenants. If you start poking around, the tenants may think that the owner is actively trying to sell the property and has concealed these plans from them. They might also think that their leaseholds are somehow in jeopardy. Throwing gasoline on landlord-tenant relations is not good for any of the parties. This will not get you off on the right foot with the owner. If you do end up owning the property, you will probably have earned the tenants' distrust.

There is no one ideal technique for approaching owners about the sale of their properties. Consider the following suggestions:

a. Make your first contact via letter. A first approach by telephone will take the owner off guard and you're likely to get an instinctive rejection. You might also be mistaken for a telemarketer and have the phone slammed in your ear.

b. Indicate something along these lines: that you're writing because you're interested in acquiring an investment property in this neighborhood and that the recipient's property is one of a small number in the area that you believe would suit your objectives. Don't exaggerate and by all means don't say anything that isn't true (e.g., "I just won the lottery and don't know what to do with my money.").

c. Do not make a specific offer.

d. Invite the owner to contact you by telephone to discuss the matter.

e. Assure the owner that you will not talk to the tenants or attempt to inspect the property until you have talked to the owner and have his or her permission to do so.

f. If you haven't heard from the owner within a week, then call on the telephone.

g. Be gracious if the owner says no. However, if you're really interested in the property, send a brief follow-up note every four to six months restating your desire to discuss its purchase.

3

Line Them Up— How to Compare Potential Investment Properties

If you can identify the price range, location, and types of properties that are candidates to purchase, then the next skill you must learn is how to identify which, if any, of these candidates you actually want to buy.

This is a crucial step. When you select a property in your comfort zone and you pay the right price for it, you maximize your chances for success. By "right price" I'm not speaking in code to suggest that you need to steal the property. If you encounter an opportunity to acquire a property below market value, that's excellent. More important is to be diligent in your analysis of the finances and of the physical property to be as certain as possible that the price you pay is fair.

In this chapter, you're going to compare properties by examining financial considerations such as income, expenses, and debt. As you might suspect, this is a topic that justifies more than a chapter. I mentioned earlier (and will again) that my earlier book—*What Every Real Estate Investor Needs to Know About Cash Flow*—is devoted entirely to the subject of financial analysis of income property. I cannot duplicate the entire contents of that book here (my publisher was very clear on this point) but I will touch on some key concepts.

Creating and comprehending financial projections about an income property is essential to your understanding of that property's current and future value as well as its performance as an investment. You can't possibly learn too much about this topic.

Let's begin with some basic concepts and definitions.

1. There is a time value to money. Cash that you receive sooner is more valuable than cash you receive later. Consider the difference between receiving $1000 today compared to $1000 five years from now. If you receive it in the future, then five years from now you will have $1000. If you receive it today, you can put it to work for you earning more cash so that five years from now you'll have more than $1000.

   For example, if you receive $1000 today and put it in the bank to earn 3 percent per year, at the end of five years you have $1159.27. You know this process as compound interest: $1000 compounded at 3 percent per year for five years.

2. The reverse of compounding is discounting. As a real estate investor you will usually look at the time value of money through the other end of the telescope. You receive the economic benefits of your investment (cash flows, as described next) not all in a big rush on day one but rather over a period of time. You receive some cash later rather than sooner, so as described in #1 above, that later cash is less valuable. As an investor you use discounting to find the Present Value of each future cash flow. The interest rate you use is now called the discount rate.

   Consider the same example as above but look at it from a different perspective. You have an investment whose worth today you do not know. You do know, however, that in five years it will pay you $1159.27. You also know that you're losing 3 percent each year and you have to wait for the payoff. What is the Present Value (i.e., the worth today) of the future cash flow? To perform this calculation manually, divide 1159.27 by 1.03; divide the result by 1.03 and repeat the process until you have done the division five times. (Note: dividing by 1.03 is a way of saying, "How much should I have had in hand, earning 3 percent to get the number I'm dividing by?") You can also go to realdata.com/secrets and download a simple Excel spreadsheet that will allow you to perform compound interest calculations.

3. When you buy an income property as an investment, what you are really buying is not a patch of dirt and a pile of lumber. You are buying what is called an income stream, i.e., a series of cash flows.

Cash Flow: All of a property's cash inflows less all its cash outflows during a given period of time. You count all money coming in whether or not it is taxable as income, and all money going out regardless of deductibility. A convention in real estate analysis is to treat all of a property's net cash flow from operation as though it occurs at one time on the last day of the year.

The first cash flow in the income stream is your initial cash investment, which occurs on the first day of the first year of your ownership (abbreviated BOY1 for "Beginning of Year 1"). Because this is money going out, it is a negative cash flow. As you operate the property, collecting rents and paying expenses, you will characterize the net cash flow each year as if it occurred on the last day (abbreviated EOY1 for "End of Year 1," EOY2, etc.). The net cash flow for any year could be positive, if you take in more than you spend, or negative if you don't.

The final cash flow during your tenure as owner occurs on the day you sell the property and receive the proceeds of that sale. You'll normally combine the sale proceeds with cash flow from operating the property into a single number, which is your cash flow for the final year.

Rule of Thumb: I cannot emphasize this enough: When you buy a piece of real estate as an income-property investment, you must view it as the purchase of an income stream. Even when some aspect of the property appears to you to be essentially a physical attribute, it's really part of your evaluation of the income stream. For example, you might feel that some of a property's value lies in its excellent location, in its extraordinary beauty and charm, or in its superb condition. You need to translate those subjective views into objective cash flow terms.

Translation #1: A property's location has a direct effect on its ability to command rent. Would you pay more rent for a view of the park or for a view of the town landfill? If you ran a retail business would you pay more for a location in the center of the shopping district or on a remote side street? The better location will create the better income stream.

Translation #2: *A property's physical appeal likewise has a direct effect on its ability to command rent. Would a law office be willing to pay more rent for a beautiful converted Victorian or for a cement-block bunker?*

Translation #3: *The fact that a property is in excellent shape obviously means you don't have to dump a lot of money in right away to bring it up to par. But if it's also clear that the current owner has always kept up the property, that fact has other implications. Good maintenance implies good management. Bad management leads to disputes with tenants, withheld rent, high vacancy, and the purchase of large quantities of antacid, all of which cost money. Think income stream.*

If you buy a piece of income-producing real estate as an investment, then these cash flow numbers are of vital importance to you. When you look at several properties you might consider purchasing, one exercise you want to perform early in the process is to compare their current and projected cash flows. To do so, you need to chart out income, expenses, and debt service.

Let's begin by using some forms that allow you to collect data about a property's income (see Figures 3.1–3.3). The reason you'll have three worksheets is because investors usually describe rental income in one of three ways: in terms of dollars per month, dollars per square foot per year, or dollars per square foot per month. Residential property is usually rented in terms of dollars per month. Often, small or single-tenant commercial spaces are also leased this way. Most other commercial space is leased on a cost-per-square-foot basis.

Rule of Thumb: *In most areas of the United States, landlords express commercial rent in terms of dollars per square foot per year, but in some parts of the country they use dollars per square foot per month. If you're not absolutely certain you know which is being represented, don't be reluctant to ask. "I assume you mean $4 per month—that's correct, isn't it?" Don't be afraid to look foolish by asking. You can't afford to guess wrong on this one.*

Property: _____

Address: _____

Contact: _____

Unit Type	Unit #	Actual $/month	Actual $/year	Market $/month	Market $/year	Proj., $/month Year 2	Proj., $/yr, Year 2	Proj., $/month Year 3	Proj., $/yr, Year 3	Proj., $/month Year 4	Proj., $/yr, Year 4	Proj., $/month Year 5	Proj., $/yr, Year 5
	1												
	2												
	3												
	4												
	5												
	6												
	7												
	8												
	9												
	10												

Other Income per mo.

Total Gross Income

FIGURE 3.1   Rent Income Summary—$ per Month.

Property: _____

Address: _____

Contact: _____

Unit Type	Unit #	Unit sf	Actual $/sf/yr	Actual $/yr	Market $/sf/yr	Market $/yr	Proj., $/sf/yr, Year 2	Proj., $/yr, Year 2	Proj., $/sf/yr, Year 3	Proj., $/yr, Year 3	Proj., $/sf/yr, Year 4	Proj., $/yr, Year 4	Proj., $/sf/yr, Year 5	Proj., $/yr, Year 5
1														
2														
3														
4														
5														
6														
7														
8														
9														
10														

Other Income, $/sf/year

Total Gross Income

FIGURE 3.2   Rent Income Summary—$ per Square Foot per Year.

Property: _____

Address: _____

Contact: _____

Unit Type	Unit #	Unit sf	Actual $/sf/mo	Actual $/yr	Market $/sf/mo	Market $/yr	Proj., $/sf/mo, Year 2	Proj., $/yr, Year 2	Proj., $/sf/mo, Year 3	Proj., $/yr, Year 3	Proj., $/sf/m0, Year 4	Proj., $/yr, Year 4	Proj., $/sf/mo, Year 5	Proj., $/yr, Year 5
1														
2														
3														
4														
5														
6														
7														
8														
9														
10														

Other Income $/sf/per mo.

Total Gross Income

FIGURE 3.3   Rent Income Summary—$ per Square Foot per Month.

You can use any or all of these forms to summarize the income from a potential investment property. Use the first if the rent is expressed as dollars per month, the second if dollars per square foot per year, and the third if dollar per square foot per month.

For the sake of illustration, let's fill one out. (For the benefit of those readers who misplaced their pencils, you can go to realdata.com/secrets and download Excel files that look like each of these paper forms but will also do some of the math for you.) You're considering a small neighborhood strip center that has five stores. One of them contains 1500 rentable square feet and is leased for $20 per square foot per year. Two others contain 1200 rentable square feet; one rents for $21 per square foot per year and the other for $22. The last two spaces are 1000 square feet each and rent for $24 per square foot. In addition to the base rent, the landlord charges each tenant $2 per rentable square foot for trash removal and parking lot maintenance. You believe that the units are rented for their fair market value and also believe that you can raise the rents 2 percent per year in the future.

Use the appropriate form to figure your current and projected future gross income from this property. Here's an example of one of them (see Figure 3.4).

In the example above, I have added the $2 per square foot for trash and maintenance of the parking lot to the base rent to give the figures shown. You will typically use "Other Income" to account for items like parking fees, vending income, and matters not specific to use of the rented space. The total of revenue for the rent is called the Gross Scheduled Income, and when you add the Other Income to it, you have the Total Gross Income.

Now that you've summarized the revenue, you can move on to chart out what is essentially the real estate equivalent of a profit and loss statement. You start with the Gross Scheduled Income.

Gross Scheduled Income: The total gross income you would collect from a property if all space were rented and all rent collected.

It would be nice if you could keep all that money and call it a day. An unfortunate truth about cash flow is that it flows both ways. Money comes in but it also goes out, primarily in the form of operating expenses and debt payments. We should also account for rent that might be lost due to vacancy and to collection problems.

Property: Oak Street Center

Address: 100-140 Oak St, Oakvile, CT

Contact: Listing Broker

Unit Type	Unit #	Unit sf	Actual $/sf/yr	Actual $/yr	Market $/sf/yr	Market $/yr	Proj., $/sf/yr, Year 2	Proj., $/yr, Year 2	Proj., $/sf/yr, Year 3	Proj., $/yr, Year 3	Proj., $/sf/yr, Year 4	Proj., $/yr, Year 4	Proj., $/sf/yr, Year 5	Proj., $/yr, Year 5
1 Retail	100	1,500	22.00	33,000	22.00	33,000	22.44	33,660	22.89	34,335	23.35	35,025	23.82	35,730
2 Retail	110	1,200	23.00	27,600	23.00	27,600	23.46	28,152	23.93	28,716	24.41	29,292	24.90	29,880
3 Retail	120	1,200	24.00	28,800	24.00	28,800	24.48	29,376	24.97	29,964	25.47	30,564	25.98	31,176
4 Retail	130	1,000	26.00	26,000	26.00	26,000	26.52	26,520	27.05	27,050	27.59	27,590	28.14	28,140
5 Retail	140	1,000	26.00	26,000	26.00	26,000	26.52	26,520	27.05	27,050	27.59	27,590	28.14	28,140
6				0		0		0		0		0		0
7				0		0		0		0		0		0
8				0		0		0		0		0		0
9				0		0		0		0		0		0
10				0		0		0		0		0		0
Other Income, $/sf/year	0		0.00	0	0.00	0	0.00	0	0.00	0	0.00	0	0.00	0
Total Gross Income			23.97	141,400	23.97	141,400	24.45	144,228	24.93	147,115	25.43	150,061	25.94	153,066

FIGURE 3.4   Rent Income Summary—$ per Square Foot per Year.

27

Vacancy and Credit Loss: *That part of the Gross Scheduled Income lost due to space that lies vacant or to nonpayment of rent by tenants.*

What's left after you subtract the Vacancy and Credit Loss from the Gross Scheduled Income is called the Gross Operating Income, or Effective Gross Income.

Gross Operating Income: *The Gross Scheduled Income reduced by the Vacancy and Credit Loss. It is not the total potential income but rather the amount you expect to collect and to have available to pay operating expenses, debt service, and capital costs.*

It will be helpful to work with some forms that you can use to summarize the items we've been discussing. Before you do that, it's essential to understand what is truly a real estate operating expense and what is not.

Operating expenses are items such as real estate taxes, property insurance, repairs, maintenance, and utilities. They are expenses that are necessary to keep the income stream flowing. It is important to know that, with real estate investment, you must not include interest expense or depreciation as an operating expense. You must also not include capital improvements or other capital costs, such as leasing commissions.

Operating Expenses: *Costs, such as repairs, insurance, utilities, necessary to maintain the income stream. Interest, depreciation, and capital costs are not real estate operating expenses.*

Why the big deal about the definition of operating expense? As you'll see shortly, these costs make up part of a very important calculation that is standardized in the industry, the calculation of the property's Net Operating Income. In order to compare properties in a meaningful way, you must stick with the definitions of these financial concepts as they are used in the real estate industry.

Now let's look at a form you can use to chart out the items we've been discussing (see Figure 3.5).

The list of expense categories shown here was not handed down on a stone tablet. It will serve to jog your thinking and to help you make certain that you don't overlook anything obvious. Some properties might experience significant ongoing expense for items not even listed here—pest control, for example. Others, such as single-tenant, freestanding commercial

5-Year Property Data					
Date:					
Prepared by:					
Property:					
Year:					
INCOME					
Gross Scheduled Rent Income					
Other Income					
TOTAL GROSS INCOME					
VACANCY & CREDIT ALLOWANCE					
GROSS OPERATING INCOME					
EXPENSES					
Accounting					
Advertising					
Insurance (fire and liability)					
Janitorial Service					
Lawn/Snow					
Legal					
Licenses					
Miscellaneous					
Property Management					
Repairs and Maintenance					
Resident Superintendent					
Supplies					
Taxes					
Real Estate					
Personal Property					
Payroll					
Other					
Trash Removal					
Utilities					
Electricity					
Fuel Oil					
Gas					
Sewer and Water					
Telephone					
Other					
TOTAL EXPENSES					
NET OPERATING INCOME					
ANNUAL DEBT SERVICE					
CASH FLOW BEFORE TAXES					

FIGURE 3.5 Five-Year Property Data.

buildings may obligate the tenant to pay all expenses as a condition of the lease, so you as the landlord have none to account for here.

Rule of Thumb: *It's quite common for a commercial tenant to pay a part or all of particular operating expenses, even in a multitenant property. These are defined in the lease between the landlord and tenant and are usually called either "pass-throughs" or "CAM (common area maintenance) charges." The landlord may pay the first X number of dollars of a particular expense (called an expense stop, because that's where the owner stops paying) and pass the rest on to the tenants. Or the landlord may pay none and pass all of the cost onto the tenants. In a multitenant property, it's common to divide the expenses among the tenants pro rata based on the square footage that each tenant occupies. However, landlords can, and often do, come up with other Byzantine schemes for dividing these costs.*

If you are the landlord, you should always pay the expense yourself and oblige the tenant to reimburse you. You should never write the lease in such a way that the tenant is responsible to pay the bills directly. There is a good reason for this warning. What if the tenant is supposed to pay the property taxes but fails to do so? Will the city or county tax collector be interested in your defense that the tenant was supposed to pay? Not a chance. It is your obligation. Worse yet, consider fire insurance. You expect the tenant to pay directly. He or she does not and the building burns down. Who loses? The correct technique is to write your lease so as to provide a time for your accounting and the tenant's payment. Characterize the required payment as a form of additional rent; then if you don't receive the payment, in most jurisdictions you should have a cause of action based on unpaid rent.

As you can see, this form allows you to show more than just expenses. You can start with the Total Gross Income that you developed on the previous form. After that, you'll notice you have a line for "Vacancy and Credit Allowance." This number is an estimate, usually a percentage of the gross income. As its name suggests (and sometimes you'll see its name as "vacancy and credit loss"), it's intended to account for revenue lost due to vacancy or to rent that is uncollectible.

Rule of Thumb: Virtually every mortgage lender will expect to see this kind of vacancy allowance as part of your cash flow projections, so you should get used to it. There is no such thing as a standard allowance—the "right" number is sensitive to market conditions for that particular type of property in that location. A broker or appraiser should be able to give you some guidance. If you have no clue whatsoever and absolutely need to plug in a number immediately, a value in the range of 2 to 5 percent would be more reasonable than nothing at all.

Speaking of nothing... If you never experience a vacancy, then perhaps you're not testing the limits of your market. In other words, maybe you're not charging enough.

The form gives you an opportunity to exercise these important definitions. You have seen the top line, Total Gross Income (also called Gross Scheduled Income) and the Vacancy and Credit Loss. The difference between these is the Gross Operating Income or GOI. The Total Gross is the amount of rent that the property would generate if fully occupied and if everyone paid with good checks. The GOI is how much of that you really expect to collect.

When you subtract your total operating expenses from the Gross Operating Income, you derive a value that is essential for the understanding of any income property: the Net Operating Income (NOI).

Net Operating Income: The property's income after vacancy and expenses but before any consideration of financing or income taxes.

NOI is important because it is central to the most common method of estimating the value of an income property.

I will touch on this only briefly here because I cover it in much greater depth in *What Every Real Estate Investor Needs to Know.* Cash flow gets entangled with issues such as mortgage payments and tax liability or tax shelter. These issues are important to you as an investor, but they are specific to you—they are not intrinsic to the property itself. Look it this way: If you were selling a property, would you feel that the value should be in any way related to the length of the loan the buyer chose or to his or her tax bracket? No; those are not part of the property. NOI is net income without regard to the effects of financing or income tax. For this reason, investors and appraisers look at NOI as a key factor driving their estimate of value.

The other factor is something called the Capitalization Rate. The Capitalization Rate (or Cap Rate as it usually called) is the rate at which you discount future income to determine its present value. Real estate investors use Cap Rates to express the relationship between a property's income (specifically its NOI) and its value. I'll discuss this further in the section, "All Cash, No Cash, or Some Borrowed Money?"

In any given market at any given time, there is typically a Cap Rate that prevails among investors buying a certain type of property—office, apartments, industrial, etc. It is essentially a rate of return and you can call this a Market Cap Rate because it is market driven. If the prevailing rate for apartment buildings is 10 percent, that's what other investors are getting. When you look at a potential investment property, you expect to get at least 10 percent as well. If you don't, you'll move on until you find one that does give you a return that's in line with other properties.

The math is simple:

Value = Net Operating Income / Cap Rate

Example

If the cap rate for industrial properties in your area is 9 percent and you are looking at a property that has a Net Operating Income of $81,000, what would you estimate as the value of that property?

Value = 81,000 / 0.09 = 900,000

You can return to the form now for one last item. You've collected the rents, paid the expenses, and made your loan payments. What's left is your Cash Flow Before Taxes. Cash flow is the net result of all funds coming in and all funds going out, and you will usually look at this, as with the other items on this form, on a yearly basis. It doesn't matter if the money coming in represents income that is taxable or not; nor does it matter if the money going is tax deductible or not. All that matters is what's left.

It's possible that less than nothing will be left. You call that a negative cash flow. You might choose to call it by other names as well, but that's your business. If you have a separate checking account for your property, a negative cash flow is tantamount to an overdraft. If your property has a negative cash flow, then you must use nonproperty (e.g., personal) funds to make up the difference.

For the purists in the audience, there is another item that could affect your cash flow but, for simplicity, I've not included it in the form. Capital improvements are generally additions or more extensive renovations that enhance, not simply maintain, a property's ability to generate income. Even though you may pay for an improvement entirely in one year, you may not be able to deduct its cost in that year, but rather over a much longer useful life.

Let's look at a sample form filled out (Figure 3.6).

In Figure 3.6, you've made projections about the next five years of income, vacancy, and expenses; those, in turn, lead you to an estimate of the Net Operating Income for each of those years. Let's say that the market-driven Capitalization Rate for properties like this in your area is 11 percent. If you apply the formula above, you can estimate the value of the property in 2006:

Value = Net Operating Income / Cap Rate

Value = 29,907 / 0.11

Value = $271,882 (round to $272,000)

Comparative Property Data

The worksheets you've been using so far are designed to allow you to look at the current figures for an income property and to project them a few years into the future. Often, when you're trying to choose among several properties, you'll find it useful to line them up for a head-to-head comparison. Instead of taking one property and looking at it over several years, let's take several properties and compare their single-year performance (see Figure 3.7).

The format here is like the previous Property Data form, but I've added one additional item. You'll find a row where you can note the Capitalization Rate that each property achieves at the selling price specified. To calculate the Cap Rate, just transpose the Value formula you saw earlier.

Value = Net Operating Income / Cap Rate

Cap Rate = Net Operating Income / Value

5-Year Property Data					
Date:	12/31/2005				
Prepared by:	First Time Investors, LLC				
Property:	Incomparable Commons				
Year:	2006	2007	2008	2009	2010
INCOME					
Gross Scheduled Rent Income	53,640	54,713	55,807	56,923	58,062
Other Income	0	0	0	0	0
TOTAL GROSS INCOME	53,640	54,713	55,807	56,923	58,062
VACANCY & CREDIT ALLOWANCE	1,073	1,094	1,161	1,139	1,161
GROSS OPERATING INCOME	52,567	53,619	54,646	55,784	56,901
EXPENSES					
Accounting	250	258	265	273	281
Advertising	0	0	0	0	0
Insurance (fire and liability)	2,930	3,077	3,230	3,392	3,561
Janitorial Service	0	0	0	0	0
Lawn/Snow	740	762	785	809	833
Legal	620	639	658	678	698
Licenses	0	0	0	0	0
Miscellaneous	320	330	340	350	360
Property Management	3,840	3,955	4,074	4,196	4,322
Repairs and Maintenance	2,930	3,018	3,108	3,202	3,298
Resident Superintendent	0	0	0	0	0
Supplies	740	762	785	809	833
Taxes					
Real Estate	4,260	4,430	4,608	4,792	4,984
Personal Property	0	0	0	0	0
Payroll	0	0	0	0	0
Other	0	0	0	0	0
Trash Removal	1,860	1,916	1,973	2,033	2,094
Utilities					
Electricity	1,220	1,257	1,294	1,333	1,373
Fuel Oil	0	0	0	0	0
Gas	0	0	0	0	0
Sewer and Water	2,950	3,039	3,130	3,224	3,320
Telephone	0	0	0	0	0
Other	0	0	0	0	0
TOTAL EXPENSES	22,660	23,443	24,250	25,091	25,957
NET OPERATING INCOME	29,907	30,176	30,396	30,693	30,944
ANNUAL DEBT SERVICE	24,466	24,923	25,384	25,384	25,384
CASH FLOW BEFORE TAXES	5,441	5,253	5,012	5,309	5,560

FIGURE 3.6   Five-Year Property Data.

Comparative Property Data					
Date:					
Prepared by:					
Property:					
Price:					
INCOME					
Gross Scheduled Rent Income					
Other Income					
TOTAL GROSS INCOME					
VACANCY & CREDIT ALLOWANCE					
GROSS OPERATING INCOME					
EXPENSES					
Accounting					
Advertising					
Insurance (fire and liability)					
Janitorial Service					
Lawn/Snow					
Legal					
Licenses					
Miscellaneous					
Property Management					
Repairs and Maintenance					
Resident Superintendent					
Supplies					
Taxes					
Real Estate					
Personal Property					
Payroll					
Other					
Trash Removal					
Utilities					
Electricity					
Fuel Oil					
Gas					
Sewer and Water					
Telephone					
Other					
TOTAL EXPENSES					
NET OPERATING INCOME					
ANNUAL DEBT SERVICE					
CASH FLOW BEFORE TAXES					
CAPITALIZATION RATE					

FIGURE 3.7   Comparative Property Data.

Comparative Property Data					
Date:	12/31/2005				
Prepared by:	First-Time Investors. LLC				
Property:	125 Main	185 Main	220 Main	36 Elm	48 Elm
Price:	325,000	260,000	260,000	375,000	375,000
INCOME					
Gross Scheduled Rent Income	53,640	44,900	47,830	58,900	62,400
Other Income	0	0	0	0	0
TOTAL GROSS INCOME	53,640	44,900	47,830	58,900	62,400
VACANCY & CREDIT ALLOWANCE	1,073	898	957	1,178	1,248
GROSS OPERATING INCOME	52,567	44,002	46,873	57,722	61,152
EXPENSES					
Accounting	250	250	250	250	250
Advertising	0	0	0	0	0
Insurance (fire and liability)	2,930	2,750	2,900	3,100	3,400
Janitorial Service	0	0	0	0	0
Lawn/Snow	740	200	640	800	720
Legal	620	600	600	700	750
Licenses	0	0	0	0	0
Miscellaneous	320	300	450	800	820
Property Management	3,840	2,772	3,000	3,463	3,669
Repairs and Maintenance	2,930	2,200	2,450	2,800	3,150
Resident Superintendent	0	0	0	0	0
Supplies	740	700	700	750	825
Taxes					
Real Estate	4,260	3,350	3,985	5,100	5,850
Personal Property	0	0	0	0	0
Payroll	0	0	0	0	0
Other	0	0	0	0	0
Trash Removal	1,860	1,860	1,860	2,050	2,050
Utilities					
Electricity	1,220	1,440	1,100	2,200	2,050
Fuel Oil	0	0	0	0	0
Gas	0	0	0	0	0
Sewer and Water	2,950	2,550	2,700	3,100	3,150
Telephone	0	0	0	0	0
Other	0	0	0	0	0
TOTAL EXPENSES	22,660	18,972	20,635	25,113	26,684
NET OPERATING INCOME	29,907	25,030	26,239	32,609	34,468
ANNUAL DEBT SERVICE	24,466	17,942	17,942	29,484	29,484
CASH FLOW BEFORE TAXES	5,441	7,088	8,297	3,125	4,984
CAPITALIZATION RATE	9.20%	9.63%	10.09%	8.70%	9.19%

FIGURE 3.8 Comparative Property Data.

I've left Figure 3.7 blank so you can make usable copies. You can also get an Excel version at realdata.com/secrets. That file will do some of the math for you. Now let's take a look at a form that's filled in (Figure 3.8).

Your five potential acquisitions have asking prices that range from $260,000 to $375,000. You presume that the market cap rate, as in the earlier example, is 11 percent and that you finance about 75 percent of the purchase price at 8 percent for 20 years. You can start your evaluation by seeing how these properties might work out if you purchased each at its full asking price. Assuming you've done a careful job of collecting data about income and expenses, it's clear that 220 Main is the closest to being priced realistically because it shows a 10.09-percent cap rate, while the asking price of 36 Elm, with a cap rate of 8.70 percent, is farthest from what the market is likely to pay. A benefit of structuring your comparison this way, of course, is that you can test some different prices quite easily to see when and if you might reach a price you would consider acceptable.

Don't lose sight of the fact that this type of comparison is a good place to start to see how competing prices stack up against each other, but it doesn't tell the whole story. You still want to project income and expenses (and hence the NOI) into the future because some properties could have significantly greater upside potential than others—opportunities that won't be revealed in a one-year snapshot.

4

Don't Get Burned— Doing Your Due Diligence

You probably wouldn't purchase a used car without checking it out, so there's no reason why you should fail to look under the hood of your real estate investment either. Your choice of an income property will be based on data about its location, its income stream, and its physical attributes. It is important to be sure that you're not missing any key information and that the data you have is accurate.

In this section you're going to see some checklists that can help you keep focused on your due-diligence mission. I'll divide these reminders into three areas: demographic, financial, and physical.

Demographics

Let's start with the demographic checklist. This is the one area you want to deal with before you begin a serious search for an investment property. You may be able to find remedies for a property's ailing financial or physical health, but there's not much you can do about its location.

Assess Neighborhood Demographics

_____ Population_____

_____ Population Growth _____

_____ Age Distribution_____

_____ Income Range_____

_____ Occupational Profile _____

_____ Major Employers _____

_____ Median Home Price _____

_____ Home Value Shift _____ Increasing _____ Stable_____ Declining

_____ Age of Housing Stock _____

_____ Housing Mix _____ SF Det _____ Condo _____ 2–4 Fam _____ Apt

_____ Apartment Vacancy _____

_____ Apartment Rent (range)_____ – _____

_____ Office Vacancy_____

_____ Office Rent/sf (range) ____–____Class A ____ – ____Class B ___ – ___ Lower

_____ Retail Vacancy _____

_____ Retail Rent/sf (range) _____ – _____

_____ Retail Area Traffic Count_____

_____ Zoning _____

_____ Local Government Issues_____

_____ General Neighborhood Appearance_____

Demographics is essentially your predeal due diligence. It pertains not to a particular property you plan to buy, but rather to the location in which you plan to invest. If you're going to get involved in this neighborhood, then you'd better know what you're getting into.

As you work with this checklist, you'll be inclined to give greater attention to some items than to others, depending on the type of property you're planning to buy. Learning about the market for office space may not be your top priority if you expect to invest in residential condos. Nonetheless, if you want to be successful with any one type of property, you would be wise to learn everything you can about the overall dynamics of the area. That office market might not be irrelevant to your goals. If the market is growing, it can provide the jobs that will attract young professionals to occupy the condos you plan to purchase. In a community of people, businesses, and properties, everything is connected to everything else. The most successful investors are those who see the connections and act on them.

Make sure you keep abreast of everything you can in regard to local politics and government plans. Are there building committees in place planning the construction of new schools? That can be good news if those schools will serve the neighborhood where you invest, but they can also have a substantial impact on property taxes. Is the town considering zoning changes, perhaps to accommodate a big-box retailer? Neither your property nor its neighborhood exists in a vacuum. At the least, you need to stay informed as to what's happening and what's planned—and sometimes you may have to exercise your prerogatives as a voter and taxpayer and make your own opinion known

Don't dismiss the last item on the list, General Neighborhood Appearance, even though it may seem very subjective. As Yogi Berra was known to say, you can observe a lot just by watching. You won't have to call a psychic hotline to determine if owners and tenants take pride in their neighborhood. Finding major appliances rusting in the front yards will tell you all you need to know.

Financial Data

The next area that deserves your scrutiny concerns financial data. You can use the Verify Financial Data checklist.

Verify Financial Data

_____ Confirm Utility Costs and Other Verifiable Expenses
    _____ Electricity_____
    _____ Gas_____
    _____ Fuel Oil _____
    _____ Sewer & Water_____
    _____ Trash _____
    _____ Property Tax_____
    _____ Insurance _____
    _____ _____
    _____ _____

_____ Verify Lease Terms
    _____ Unit: _____ _____
    _____ Unit: _____ _____
    _____ Unit: _____ _____
    _____ Unit: _____ _____
    _____ Unit: _____ _____
    _____ Unit: _____ _____
    _____ Unit: _____ _____

_____ Verify Tenant Payment History
    _____ Unit: _____ _____
    _____ Unit: _____ _____
    _____ Unit: _____ _____
    _____ Unit: _____ _____
    _____ Unit: _____ _____
    _____ Unit: _____ _____
    _____ Unit: _____ _____

_____ Verify Security Deposits
    _____ Unit: _____ _____
    _____ Unit: _____ _____
    _____ Unit: _____ _____
    _____ Unit: _____ _____
    _____ Unit: _____ _____
    _____ Unit: _____ _____
    _____ Unit: _____ _____

_____ Verify Tax Returns (Partnership of Schedule E)
    _____ Year: _____ _____
    _____ Year: _____ _____
    _____ Year: _____ _____

_____ Verify Other Contracts in Place
    _____ Property Mgmt _____
    _____ _____
    _____ _____

_____ Verify Insurance Policies _____
_____ Recent Insurance Claims _____
_____ Verify Title Policies _____

Again, the list should serve as a memory jog, not as an exhaustive catalog of financial issues. While assessing neighborhood demographics is something you should do *before* you identify individual properties you might purchase, do not expect to get too far along in the process of financial verification until you are closer to making a deal. As a practical matter, you shouldn't spend the time necessary to check all this information in regard to a property that you merely have under consideration. You'll end up like Hamlet and never get the job done. Unless you have a purchase contract under negotiation, you're unlikely to gain access to much of this information anyway. No seller is going to show his or her tax returns and leases to a tire kicker.

> ***Rule of Thumb:*** *Your best approach is to make your offer to purchase subject to verification and approval of the relevant items on this list. You definitely want to see all leases as well as information about security deposits and copies of contracts that are in place. Reviewing tenant payment histories can give you a heads-up on potential problems Ask to see the current insurance policy and insist on knowing about claims in the past five years. When you kick over a rock, you never know what might scamper out.*
>
> *There is an especially important reason why you need to know about past insurance claims. If the property has experienced a claim for water damage within the past years, you could find it very difficult and expensive to obtain liability insurance for it. The apparent reason is fear of mold. Insurers have become increasingly gun-shy about the number and size of claims and large awards related to the health consequences of mold. It may sound absurd that the destruction of a hardwood floor by a clothes washer gone berserk could be such a big deal. Yet that's exactly the issue I encountered recently. Because of one errant load of laundry, I spent weeks searching and ended up paying almost three times as much as I had previously for insurance. You might discuss with your attorney including in your purchase contract a warranty by the seller that there has been no water damage and no water- or mold-related claims within the past five years.*
>
> *Specify a period of time after you receive documents from the seller—perhaps a month—during which you can review them, and be certain to stipulate that you can call the deal off if there is any-*

thing about your due diligence that doesn't satisfy you—including lack of cooperation by the seller.

You must take these verifications seriously. I have seen more than one occasion where the truth emerged only after being pried loose by a clause in a purchase agreement. In my own experience, the most common fantasy has occurred in the quoting of residential rents. Sellers seemed to hear voices that told them what they *should* be getting for rent and somehow that became their new reality.

Examining and approving the leases and verifying tenant security deposits are two conditions of purchase that you must treat as nonnegotiable. Once you take over as owner, you are bound by the terms of those leases so you must know what they say. Read them carefully and don't assume that what looks like boilerplate is either consistent or harmless. Have your attorney read them as well.

Regarding deposits, remember that, if the tenants fulfill their obligations, then you will be required to return their deposits. It's essential to know the correct amounts and to be certain that they are turned over to you at closing. Also find out if interest payable to the tenants has accrued on the deposits and if so, make sure you collect it from the seller at closing.

> **Rule of Thumb:** *Tax returns—or at least relevant tax return schedules, such as "E"—can tell you a great deal if you can get them. The seller will balk; remind him or her that you want only the pages that pertain to the property. It's highly improbable that a property owner will overstate income or understate expenses on a tax return, so if the information on the return doesn't match the data represented by the seller or broker, you want an explanation. If part of that explanation is—"Sometimes they pay in cash and I never report that, but of course you can count on it as rent, no problem"—then run like the wind. Do you really expect that everything else he has said about the property is true? Are you willing to bet your life's savings on it?*

Physical Inspection

Throughout this book I emphasize that a real estate investment is the purchase of an income stream rather than the purchase of a physical asset. I restate this point so often because you probably find it to be a counterintuitive concept. The truth, of course, is that the emperor really does have new clothes: There is a real parcel of land with a tangible structure on it. If the physical asset is in good condition, then the income stream can flourish; if it's in poor condition, the stream can dry up. A property that presents you with substantial, unexpected repair costs will quickly deplete your cash flow and reduce that property's investment value.

How do you know if a property is in good shape? Kicking the tires won't tell you anything about a car, and the same amateurish approach won't help you with land or buildings. I must deal another blow to the rugged individualists among you: Unless you're trained to inspect properties, you're not likely to pick up on more than the superficial problems. You need to hire professionals for this job.

A good place to begin looking is among the membership of the American Society of Home Inspectors (ashi.org). If your property is a single-family or small multifamily, you should have no difficulty finding a number of candidates to do the job. Many states now require licensing for this profession, and ASHI members subscribe to the organization's code of ethics and standards of practice. If your property is commercial, you may still find a suitable choice here because some companies inspect all property types. A commercial broker or your local chamber of commerce may also be able to refer a building engineering firm. (See the Inspection Checklist.)

Do not use this list to survey the property by yourself. Read the report you receive from a professional inspector or engineer. Extract from that report the issues you might need to deal with and use the form to summarize those. In other words, boil the report down to items that require action and use the form to keep you focused on those.

Keep in mind that every property has imperfections and not all imperfections need to be remedied. Some of the exterior walls of my home are visibly out of plumb. The house has remained standing for almost 150 years, so I feel no need to spend a fortune trying to solve what is not really a problem. I just use Velcro® when I hang pictures. You need to apply some judgment to the issues that an inspection report inevitably will raise. Some could be deal-killers. With others, the cost of the remedy is something you can negotiate with the seller. Still others might be inconsequential.

Inspection Checklist

_____ Building

     _____ Construction type (frame, masonry) _____

     _____ Exterior walls (type & condition) _____

     _____ Roof (type & condition) _____

     _____ Foundation (type & condition) _____

     _____ Floors and flooring _____

     _____ Interior walls (type & condition) _____

     _____ Windows _____

     _____ Chimneys _____

     _____ Plumbing & fixtures _____

     _____ Electrical & fixtures _____

     _____ Water & sewer _____

     _____ HVAC, oil tanks _____

     _____ Doors & hardware _____

     _____ Kitchens _____

     _____ Bathrooms _____

     _____ Security _____

     _____ Fire protection _____

     _____ Sewer & Water _____

     _____ Elevators _____

     _____ Lobbies, public restrooms _____

     _____ Pest infestations _____

_____ Site

     _____ Environmental assessment _____

     _____ Landscaping _____

     _____ Drainage _____

     _____ Paving _____

     _____ Sidewalks & curbs _____

     _____ Outside lighting _____

     _____ Trash receptacles _____

     _____ _____

     _____ _____

     _____ _____

     _____ _____

Speaking of deal-killers, turn your attention to the item, "environmental assessment." You will generally need to engage a separate company to perform what is called a "Phase I Environmental Assessment." The purpose is to look for hazards such as asbestos, PCBs, radon, underground storage tanks, lead-based paint, and contamination from waste sites. An asbestos collar on a heating pipe is not a major item to deal with, but serious contamination is a nightmare that won't go away easily. If the property you're purchasing is commercial, your lender will almost certainly insist on a Phase I survey. If anything smells fishy (figuratively or otherwise), you'll have to do a more expensive and elaborate Phase II. Cleaning up a contaminated property can be a costly business and sometimes—with ground contamination particularly—it can be difficult to estimate the extent of the problem until remediation begins. Some problems, such as lead paint or the minimal presence of asbestos can often be resolved at a fixed and manageable cost, but if you're a beginning investor, leave Pandora's box closed and stay away from properties that have serious environmental issues.

Legal Issues

We've been making good use of checklists in this chapter, so I'll supply yet another here. The purpose of this list, however, is not to provide you with a personal action plan but rather with the rough outline of an agenda.

In reality, there is only one legal issue you have to deal with: finding a good attorney, someone who specializes in real estate transactions. If there were a time in our discourse to flash the "Don't Try This at Home" warning label, this would be it. The legal issues that inhabit real estate transactions are sufficiently arcane that you need an expert to serve both as counsel and watchdog. The Legal Checklist includes items you should expect to discuss with your attorney as the transaction progresses.

Let's discuss some of these items. The basic terms of the deal include purchase price and earnest money deposit. Virtually every real estate contract will also include contingencies. First among these is typically a clause that makes your obligation to complete the purchase subject to your ability to secure financing upon certain terms and within a specified period of time. A second condition you want to include allows you to conduct a complete engineering inspection of the property and to walk away from the deal

Legal Checklist

_____ Purchase Contract

    _____ Purchase terms: _____

    _____ Financing contingencies:_____ _____

    _____ Inspection contingencies: _____

    _____ Seller representations: _____

    _____ Leases, estoppel certificates:_____

    _____ Tenant deposits: _____

    _____ Other due diligence: _____

    _____ Seller guarantees:_____

    _____ Closing date: _____

    _____ Inventory, property & equip.: _____

    _____ _____

_____ Marketable title: _____

_____ Easements: _____

_____ Survey: _____

_____ Zoning compliance: _____

_____ Building code compliance:_____

_____ Lien waivers: _____

_____ Subject to contracts:_____

_____ _____

_____ _____

if there is anything you don't like about the results. It's also common to add language to a contract that obliges the seller to reveal any known but hidden defects—i.e., defects that an inspection might not reveal.

The contract should also do as much as possible to pin down the accuracy of representations made by the seller or the broker. One of the best ways to accomplish this is with something called an Estoppel Certificate. This certificate is provided not by the landlord but by each tenant in the property. A good commercial lease will obligate the tenant to complete such a certificate if requested. There is no standard format, but what it should include is a statement from the tenant verifying the following:

1. The location and size of the leased space
2. The starting and expiration dates of the lease
3. Any options to renew and the terms thereof
4. The amount of the rent (including escalations)
5. The status of rent payments (current or past due)
6. The presence of any defaults by the landlord
7. The amount of security deposits
8. The status of any tenant improvements promised by the landlord
9. Any rights of first refusal
10. Any option to expand the leased space

If you have negotiated any guarantees with the seller, you should have those recited in the contract as well. For example, you ask the seller to promise not to enter into any new lease agreements prior to the closing without your consent. (Picture this: You close the deal, only to find that the seller has just installed his girlfriend in an apartment with what is literally a sweetheart lease. Bada Bing!) You might also negotiate the deal so that, if any now-occupied unit becomes vacant before the closing, then the seller agrees to pay that rent for a specified number of months. Whatever the seller has promised to do should be spelled out in the contract.

Another matter that should be itemized is an inventory of any personal property or equipment that is to be conveyed with the property. With apartment buildings, for example, there may be appliances in the units and coin-op laundry machines in a common area.

Other legal issues may require attention as well. Your attorney should determine if the seller has a clear and marketable title to convey, whether there are any easements you should be aware of, and whether the property is in fact zoned for its current or intended use. If there was any recent construction activity, you should obtain lien waivers from all contractors who might otherwise have claims against the property for unpaid work.

Just as you are obligated to honor the leases when you become the new owner, you may also be obligated to honor other contracts as well. There might be a property management contract in place or service agreements for security systems, elevators, sprinklers, trash removal, pest control, lawn care, snow removal, or janitorial service. If you have a duty to maintain these contracts, then you need to know what they entail.

A final word: It's easy to take things for granted or to take them at face value. "Due diligence takes too much time, too much effort, too much money; let's just spot-check the high points and be done with it, OK?" No. Don't skimp on your due diligence. Matters are not always what they seem, and if what you buy turns out to be a surprise package—a property with environmental issues, a serious structural defect, or tenants in revolt—correcting the problem can take a great deal more time, effort, and money than some prepurchase prudence.

PART 2

FINANCING YOUR INVESTMENT PROPERTY

Types, Terms, and Sources of Loans

Love might make the world go 'round, but it's financing that makes real estate deals spin like a top. It may be a sweeping generalization, but true nonetheless, that if you don't succeed at obtaining financing, you won't succeed as a real estate investor.

In this section you'll learn about different types of loans and the kinds of terms and conditions that may accompany them. You also learn a little about the different types of lenders who can finance your deals.

Every business and profession has its own special jargon, and real estate is certainly no exception. You'll exit this chapter with a whole new collection of terms that you can use at cocktail parties, or wherever. Because the topic of this section is financing, let's start with the term, "mortgage." You go to the bank or to some other lender to get money in the form of a mortgage loan or mortgage financing, evidenced by a mortgage note. In return for their largesse, you give the lender a lien against the property, called a mortgage or mortgage deed or deed of trust. Hence, our first financing related definition:

> ***Mortgage:*** *A security instrument in which real property is pledged as collateral for the payment of an accompanying mortgage note.*

There are many types of mortgage loans as well as many conditions that may be included in the mortgage note. The most common structure is the level-payment, amortizing loan. The note for such a loan is comprised of four basic terms:

1. **Principal amount**—This is the amount of money you borrow. It can also refer to the amount you still owe after making payments for a given period of time.
2. **Term**—This is the length of the loan. You will typically make payments to the lender over time. At the end of the term, you will have repaid all of the principal plus some amount of interest as a fee for use of the money. You'll make payments "periodically," with the most common period being monthly, but the note could define the payment period as biweekly, quarterly, semiannually, or annually.
3. **Interest rate**—You are accustomed to seeing the interest rate for a mortgage loan expressed as the annual rate (for example, 9 percent per year) even though you will probably not be making annual payments. For purposes of understanding how a loan works, you should think in terms of its *Periodic Interest Rate*, i.e., the rate per payment period. For example, if you have a 9-percent loan on which you make monthly payments, then the Periodic Interest Rate is one-twelfth of 9 percent or 0.75 percent. This is the rate you would use to determine the amount of interest you would owe for the use of the lender's money for one payment period, i.e., one month.

   You undoubtedly have heard the term *Annual Percentage Rate (APR)*. That expression is used for disclosure purposes only and has no relevance to the loan calculations you'll perform. Federal Regulation Z requires lenders to estimate a loan's effective interest rate, taking into account certain loan fees (such as points) and assumptions that interest rates on adjustable-rate loans will rise over time.
4. **Periodic Payment**—This is the amount you pay each period. In a level-payment loan, you pay the same amount each period and that amount typically includes some principal and some interest. By the time you reach the last payment of the prescribed term, you will have paid back the entire principal.

   As you'll see below, a mortgage loan can have payments that are not level. A simple example is a situation where you agree to pay only interest for a specified number of periods (not reducing the principal balance at all) and then pay off the principal in one lump sum, usually through a refinance with another lender.

You can divide mortgage loans for real estate investment and development into two broad types. The first type is the conventional loan. This is a loan you would obtain from an institutional lender, such as a bank or insurance company. Presumably, you would call the other type "unconventional," but that label suggests that there is something peculiar about such loans. (I get a mental picture of a loan officer wearing a tie-dyed shirt and mirrored sunglasses.) Let's call these loans nonconventional. You could obtain this type of loan from a private investment group, from the seller of the property, or even from your Uncle Harry.

Conventional Mortgage Loan: *A loan obtained from an institutional source, such as a bank or insurance company.*

What makes conventional lenders conventional is that they exhibit some general uniformity in their underwriting standards—uniformity driven by banking regulations and/or shareholders' expectation of sound business practices. Do not interpret "general uniformity" to mean cookie-cutter standardization. One conventional lender may routinely loan up to 80 percent of the value of apartment buildings while another sets a limit of 75 percent; one lender may require a Debt Coverage Ratio of 1.20; another, 1.30. In a given regional market, you're not likely to see huge differences among conventional lenders in regard to their underwriting standards.

Debt Coverage Ratio: *The ratio of a property's Net Operating Income (Gross Scheduled Income less Vacancy and Credit Loss less Operating Expenses) to the Annual Debt Service (total annual mortgage payments). A DCR of 1.00 means you have just enough net income to make your mortgage payments. A DCR of 1.20 means you expect to have 20 percent more net income than needed to pay the mortgage—in other words, a cushion.*

Once a conventional lender has closed a mortgage loan transaction, it will either keep that loan in-house or sell it on what is called the secondary mortgage market. If you have ever financed the purchase of a personal residence using a bank or Savings and Loan institution, then you have almost certainly dealt with a lender that sells its loan on the secondary market. By doing so, the lender can replenish its lending resources and continue to make new loans to new borrowers.

The secondary market for residential properties of up to four units consists primarily of FNMA (Fannie Mae) and FHLMC (Freddie Mac), two privately owned but government-sponsored enterprises. These organizations buy loans from conventional lenders, holding some and securitizing others for sale to investors.

In order for a lender to sell a loan to Fannie Mae or Freddie Mac, the loan must conform to the underwriting requirements of these organizations. (You may have heard the term "conforming loan" mentioned by a lender; it refers to a loan that abides by these underwriting conditions.) The requirements include maximum loan amount (adjusted frequently to reflect the rising cost of housing) and maximum Loan-to-Value ratio. Loan applications and appraisal reports must also use approved FNMA/FHLMC forms.

So-called conduit lenders also sell loans to private investment houses, who package these loans into Collateralized Mortgage Backed Securities (CMBS). Conduit lenders usually deal with loans starting at or above $1 million (as of this writing). Because the loan usually gets sliced and diced as part of a package that contains certain yield guarantees, the borrower may face both a lock-out period of three to five years during which he or she cannot retire the loan by sale or refinance, and a prepayment penalty for a time thereafter.

> *Rule of Thumb: Conduit loans are an important part of the commercial finance industry, but they're not for beginners. The complexity and restrictive features of conduit loans can make them a difficult environment in which to learn the business.*

Some lenders retain their loans in-house, and these are called "Portfolio Lenders." Because they don't sell their loans, they don't have to conform to anyone's underwriting standards but their own. Don't take that to mean they have diluted standards or that they differ dramatically from other sources of financing. You'll find their underwriting requirements to be quite similar to those of conventional lenders. What distinguishes them is their flexibility; in other words, their lending guidelines tend to be similar but not as rigid as those of institutions who sell their loans. You have a good chance of developing a working relationship over time with a portfolio lender. As you demonstrate your competence, you can bring in a square peg and work out a way to fit it in the round hole—"I want to purchase this vacant building, rehab it, add first-floor retail, convert the upper floors to condos, keep some, and rent the rest. Can you finance that?"

Portfolio Lender: A lender that keeps loans in-house (i.e., in its own portfolio) rather than selling them to investors.

As a rule, a loan from a portfolio lender is likely to carry a slightly higher interest rate or shorter term than a loan from a nonportfolio lender. If you keep your eye on the bigger picture, the added cost may be worthwhile. Time, as you may have heard, is money. It can take time and effort to search for and secure financing. A good working relationship that accelerates the process can, in the long run, be worth more than the extra loan costs.

You can also seek financing through a mortgage broker. The broker doesn't actually lend money. Instead, he or she acts as a representative of the wholesale divisions of a number of lenders. The broker has access to wholesale rates and marks these up to earn a fee. Using a broker can have advantages. First, you deal with one person who in turn can shop your requirements among several lenders or identify one who is particularly well suited for your deal. Second, the broker knows how to present the information in your application in a format that the lender prefers.

Mortgage Broker: An individual or firm that represents a variety of lenders and arranges real estate financing for borrowers. When the loan closes, the broker is paid a fee by the lender or borrower.

Mortgage brokers are like the little girl of Mother Goose fame with a curl in the middle of her forehead. When they're good, they're very, very good; and when they're bad, they're horrid. The good ones will find financing that you might never discover on your own. The horrid ones tack on enough fees to sink a barge. Also, the explosive growth of refinancing that was prompted by low interest rates has attracted into the business some people with minimal qualifications. Get references or look for a referral from a commercial real estate broker or another investor.

Rule of Thumb: I repeat the earlier axiom: Your success as an investor will depend on your ability to obtain mortgage financing. Cultivate a good working relationship with a lender or broker. If you can't identify a suitable broker or portfolio lender, try a local bank or S&L—someone you can get to know. Keep in mind that the relationship has value. It is better to build that relationship than to save ¼ percent on a loan by running all over the state.

Nonconventional mortgage loan: *A loan obtained from a private source, such as the seller of the property.*

A private lender and a borrower can usually strike any deal they want as long as it is not so predatory that is violates usury laws (which, of course, vary from state to state). So if the seller wants to loan you 100 percent of the purchase price, she can.

So-called "hard money lenders" are private individuals or groups of investors who provide financing that the borrower can't obtain from a conventional source. For example, you might not have enough cash for the down payment on a property. Or the property's cash flow might not meet conventional underwriting standards, yet you are determined to complete the purchase anyway. Hard-money lenders take on deals that conventional lenders find too risky. Risk equals cost, so you can expect to pay a premium for this type of loan.

A loan from a property seller may or may not be a wise move. A lot depends on your ability to discern the seller's real motives in offering the loan. It might be that he or she is faced with a substantial capital gain on a property that has been fully depreciated. The seller can ameliorate that problem with an installment sale, spreading receipt of the gain (and the tax liability) over time. In this case, you're doing the seller a favor, so the private financing should not contain onerous terms (unless, of course, you're a terrible credit risk). On the other hand, the seller might have convinced you to accept an inflated price for the property and knows that the property will never pass an independent bank appraisal at that price.

The kinds of nonconventional financing I've discussed here are fairly straightforward. However, there are plenty of more exotic loan structures—equity sharing, cash flow participations, wraparounds, graduated payments—limited only by the imaginations of the parties involved. Some can be very effective at getting the job done but can also be fraught with pitfalls. By way of example, let's look at two types of loans that you might use if you were seeking financing from the seller.

Graduated Payment Mortgage

If the seller is in a position to take back all of the financing you need and is very motivated to make the deal, he or she might be willing to work out some variation of a Graduated Payment Mortgage. Essentially, this is a loan in which the monthly payments begin well below what would be necessary for a level-payment, amortizing loan, an amount that is not even sufficient to cover the interest that should accrue with each payment. The shortfall is added on to the outstanding principal balance each month. Initially, the loan balance goes up because of this "negative amortization." However, the loan is also structured so that the payment amount increases regularly, usually each year up to a predefined level. With each increase in payment, there is less negative amortization; then no negative effect; and finally an increasingly positive amortization. It reaches a level that allows the loan to amortize fully within the originally prescribed term.

The purpose of this type of loan is to minimize the debt service and hence maximize the cash flow in the early years. There might be acceptable reasons why you need this help to cover the cash flow. You might be inheriting below-market leases that will expire in a few years. You have to deal with that reality but are confident you can improve the cash flow and create significant value afterward, when you bring the income up to market levels. There are, of course, more ominous possibilities why you would need such a device to offset a weak cash flow: You might be overpaying for the property or leveraging it too high, i.e., not using enough of your own cash.

Essentially what you are doing with the negative amortization is borrowing more money each month at the interest rate of the loan. This is not necessarily bad, but it does represent a situation where you need to do some careful projections. Will the interest costs on this additional borrowing deplete the overall return on this property so that it's no longer a worthwhile investment? Or will the cash-flow assistance from reduced debt service make it possible for you actually to do the deal, a deal whose substantial payday when you sell justifies the cost? There are no set answers to these questions. It all depends on the purchase price of the property, your cash investment, the terms of the loan, the projected cash flow, and the ultimate resale value—exactly the same as it would if you were using completely conventional financing. Here, as in a conventional transaction, you should lay the numbers out in black and white to see if they make sense.

A number of banks have begun to offer adjustable-rate loans with graduated payments as an option. See the discussion of "Option-ARMs," below.

Wraparound Mortgage

Another type of loan that might be suitable for seller financing is the wrap-around mortgage. In this transaction the seller has an existing mortgage on the property. Instead of paying this loan off, he or she "wraps" a new loan around it—that is, creates a new, larger loan that is subordinate to the existing first mortgage. The buyer of the property makes payments to the seller on the wraparound and the seller continues to make payments to the first mortgage lender on the smaller original loan. One of the motivations that a seller might have to do this is if this existing loan is at a significantly lower rate than he can charge to the new buyer. The seller will collect payments on a larger mortgage at a higher rate while continuing to pay on the smaller mortgage at the lower rate. Another motivation, of course, is that the seller's ability to provide financing is what makes the deal possible for the buyer.

A frequent fly in this particular ointment is the likelihood of a "due on sale" clause in the underlying mortgage note. Such a clause requires that the loan must be retired if the borrower transfers title to the property. Not all mortgage notes contain such a clause, but most do. A method that sellers have used to address this problem is something called a "contract for deed." This is an installment sale where title doesn't actually pass to the buyer until the seller is fully paid off—that is, until the wraparound mortgage is paid. The first mortgage holder may not agree with this reasoning and see this transaction as a sale. This is a sufficiently gray area that you, either as buyer or seller, should definitely seek legal counsel before attempting a contract for deed.

Even without the due on sale clause, there are enough issues wrapped up in a wraparound mortgage that you need the services of an attorney with experience in setting up such a deal. The seller needs to impound money for property taxes and insurance, just as an institutional lender would. The buyer needs protection that the seller will continue to pay the original mortgage and not do anything that might cloud the property's title.

Rule of Thumb: If you're brand new to real estate investing, you should lean toward more-or-less conventional financing for your first deal. This advice is not the kind that makes for a good infomercial—perhaps that's why you haven't seen me on late-night cable TV recently. Get your first loan from an S&L or commercial bank, through a mortgage broker, or perhaps in a straight-up note from the seller, but eschew the temptation to jump right away into overly creative financing.

If you signed up for tennis lessons, you probably wouldn't be pleased if the instructor started off teaching you trick shots before showing you the basic backhand and forehand. Be at least as sensible in your approach to financing your investment property. Creative loans can be very effective deal-makers, but they can also pose risks for the novice. After you've built up some experience and a sense of what works, what doesn't, and what makes the warning lights flash, you can then venture out into more exotic financing methods. I know. I sound like your mother. So don't play with your food either.

Loan Terms and Conditions

A mortgage loan is a contract and, like every contract, contains certain terms and conditions. Earlier in this section you saw the four basic elements of a loan: principal amount, term (i.e., the length of the loan), periodic interest rate, and periodic payment. These four items interact with each other mathematically. Beyond the basic math, however, each of the four items plays an important role in the overall structure of the loan:

Principal

In a later section of this book you'll find a quasiphilosophical/mathematical discussion of how much you *should* borrow—all, some, or none of the purchase price. Still elsewhere you'll see a more practical discourse on how much you **can** expect to borrow against a particular property. I won't repeat either of those discussions here but from whichever end you approach the matter, you can expect that the first question your lender will ask of you is, "How much?"

The principal amount is your starting point for a new loan. In a typical loan a portion of each of your payments is applied to interest and the rest is applied to the outstanding principal balance, reducing that balance bit by bit until you have retired it entirely. This process of principal reduction is called "amortization."

Consider this example: You have a brand new $100,000 mortgage loan at 12 percent per year payable in 240 monthly installments of $1101.09 (see Figure 5.1). The annual interest rate of 12 percent equates to 1 percent per month, so you must pay exactly $1000 (1 percent of 100,000) interest for your use of the money in the first month. The balance of your first payment, $101.09, is applied to the principal, reducing the amount you owe to $99,898.91. In the second month, you need to pay 1-percent interest ($998.99) on this new lower balance, so there is more of the payment left over ($102.10) to apply to the principal. With each passing month, the balance shifts at a glacial pace in favor of principal until eventually your loan is paid off.

If you pay off your loan before it is fully amortized—a sale or refinance being the most likely reasons—then you will need to know the principal balance at that interim point. You can go to my company's Web site, realdata.com, and download the RealData® Calculator, a Windows®-based program that allows you to perform all sorts of real-estate-related computations. We distribute the calculator free of charge. With one of the modules you can print what is called an amortization schedule, a month-by-month table that shows the interest and principal components of each payment, the

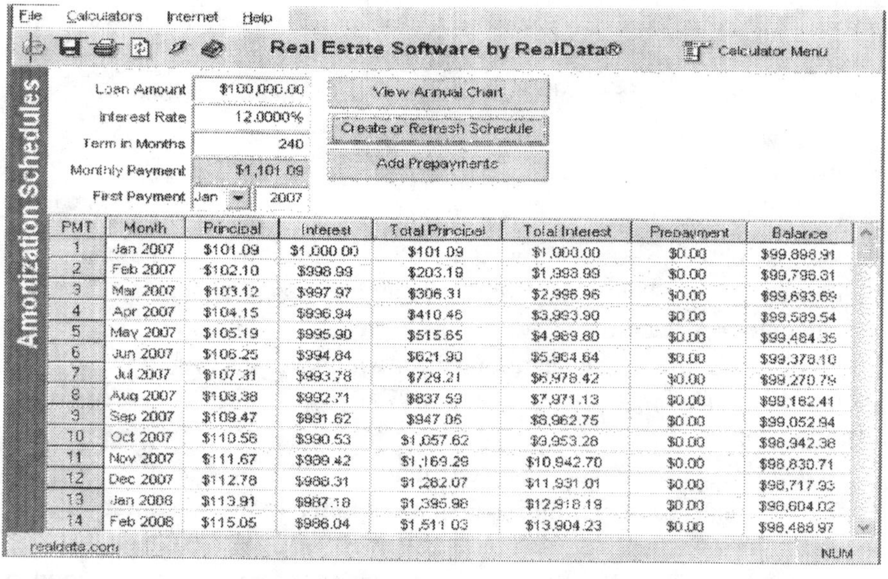

PMT	Month	Principal	Interest	Total Principal	Total Interest	Prepayment	Balance
1	Jan 2007	$101.09	$1,000.00	$101.09	$1,000.00	$0.00	$99,898.91
2	Feb 2007	$102.10	$998.99	$203.19	$1,998.99	$0.00	$99,796.81
3	Mar 2007	$103.12	$997.97	$306.31	$2,996.96	$0.00	$99,693.69
4	Apr 2007	$104.15	$996.94	$410.46	$3,993.90	$0.00	$99,589.54
5	May 2007	$105.19	$995.90	$515.65	$4,989.80	$0.00	$99,484.35
6	Jun 2007	$106.25	$994.84	$621.90	$5,984.64	$0.00	$99,378.10
7	Jul 2007	$107.31	$993.78	$729.21	$6,978.42	$0.00	$99,270.79
8	Aug 2007	$108.38	$992.71	$837.59	$7,971.13	$0.00	$99,162.41
9	Sep 2007	$109.47	$991.62	$947.06	$8,962.75	$0.00	$99,052.94
10	Oct 2007	$110.56	$990.53	$1,057.62	$9,953.28	$0.00	$98,942.38
11	Nov 2007	$111.67	$989.42	$1,169.29	$10,942.70	$0.00	$98,830.71
12	Dec 2007	$112.78	$988.31	$1,282.07	$11,931.01	$0.00	$98,717.93
13	Jan 2008	$113.91	$987.18	$1,395.98	$12,918.19	$0.00	$98,604.02
14	Feb 2008	$115.05	$986.04	$1,511.03	$13,904.23	$0.00	$98,488.97

FIGURE 5.1 Screen Shot from the RealData® Calculator (Amortization Schedule) Available at www.realdata.com.

interest paid to date, and the outstanding principal balance. The snippet of an amortization schedule shown in Figure 5.1 is taken from that program.

Sometimes loans are structured in a way that the payment does not in fact reduce the outstanding debt. For example, if the monthly payment on the loan above were exactly $1000 it would be sufficient to cover the interest, but there would be nothing left over to reduce the principal. With no principal reduction, the interest due in month 2 would again be $1000. With this arrangement the loan would never be amortized and would have to be paid off with a "balloon" as discussed below.

What if the payment on this loan were set at $600? Now there is not even enough to pay the interest. In this case the monthly shortfall must be added on to the amount you owe. You need $1000 to pay the interest for month one; you deliver only $600, so you are $400 short. That $400 is added to the balance, so at the end of month one you owe $100,400. Next month you'll owe $1004 in interest so you'll be $404 short. Instead of going down each month, your outstanding principal balance is going up—a process known oxymoronically as "negative amortization." Once again you'll need a balloon payment to retire the loan.

Interest

Like auto manufacturers, lenders seem to come up with new models for interest rates almost every year. Your next loan might even have cup holders and a global navigation system. Some of the standard loan choices du jour are...

1. **Fixed-rate mortgage**—The simplest to describe; whatever rate you start with is the rate you will keep for the life of the loan. Risk always has a cost, and the risk to the lender is that it will be locked into your low-rate loan at some future time when it could lend that money at a higher rate. Hence, on any given day, you will pay more for a fixed-rate loan than you would for a loan whose rate can vary.
2. **Adjustable-rate mortgage (ARM)**—In general, a loan whose rate can change from time to time. The parameters are enough to make a grown investor dizzy; I'll try to sort some of them out:

   How: In relation to an index. The loan might start off at an especially low teaser rate, but thereafter the new rate will adjust to some percentage above or below a given index—the prime rate, Constant Maturity Treasury (CMT), 11th District Cost of Funds Index (COFI) and London Interbank Offer Rate (LIBOR), and the Monthly Treasury Average (MTA) are the most common.

The 1-year CMT, more commonly called the 1-year T-Bill index, is used with the majority of adjustable-rate mortgages. It is fairly volatile and reacts quickly to changes in economic conditions. The LIBOR index, which is based on the interest rate that certain London Banks charge each other, is similarly quick to react to economic changes.

Most lines of credit, including home equity loans, business loans, and some commercial mortgages are tied to the prime rate. It tends to be less volatile than the T-Bill.

The COFI index is tied to interest paid on savings accounts and tends to move fairly slowly. Another slow mover is the MTA, which reflects a rolling 12-month average of the yield on U.S. Treasury securities.

Rule of Thumb: Loans related to the COFI and MTA indices are generally good choices if you believe interest rates will be rising over time. That's because they tend to lag behind the market and will rise more slowly than the other indices. By the same reasoning, they're less attractive choices if you think rates will trend downward because they won't drop as quickly as others. In that situation, you would prefer T-Bill or LIBOR indexed loans.

How often: If the interest rate is described as floating, then it can change whenever the index rate (for example, the prime rate) changes. Otherwise, the note will specify that the rate can change periodically, usually every 1 to 12 months.

How much: The loan will usually cite a maximum amount that the rate can change with any single adjustment (for example, 2 percent) as well as a rate ceiling and sometimes a rate floor for the life of the loan.

3. **Fixed to ARM**—Provides a fixed rate for a given number of years, usually 1, 3, 5, or 7; then becomes an ARM for the balance of its term.
4. **5/25, 7/23**—Like the fixed-to-arm, but actually a fixed-to-fixed. Provides one fixed rate for the first portion of the term, then adjusts to a new rate that remains constant for the remaining years.

5. **Interest Only**—This type of loan was once encountered mostly in secondary or short-term financing, but has become part of more mainstream loan programs. You'll now find interest-only offered by institutional lenders, even on home loans. This can be an effective tool for an investor. One way to look at the amortization that occurs with a standard loan is as a sort of forced and illiquid form of savings.

   Rule of Thumb: If the investment property you're dealing with throws off a marginal or negative cash flow, you might feel more comfortable holding on to what otherwise would have been the principal portion of your mortgage payment. You always have the option of paying the lender more and having that additional amount applied to the reduction of principal. With an amortizing mortgage, however, you don't have the option of going the other way and paying just the interest.

6. **Option ARM**—These loans go by several names and are often linked to the Cost of Funds Index (COFI). This is a type of Graduated Payment Mortgage as I discussed above where the monthly payment amount starts very low—i.e., not even enough to coverage the interest due—so the shortfall is added onto the loan balance in a process called negative amortization. In the typical structure, the borrower can elect each month to make this minimum payment or can choose to pay a full interest-only amount or even an amount that would equal the payment on a 30- or 15-year amortizing loan. That's the "option" part of the Option ARM.

   In the typical version of this loan, the interest rate can adjust monthly, up or down; but each year the minimum payment increases by 7.5 percent (it's the *payment* that increases by this percentage, not the loan's interest rate). By having the payment amount graduate over time, the loan starts off with atypically low payments, making it easier to qualify for and easier to manage initially. Eventually the annually increasing payment moves the loan into positive amortization so that it does in fact get paid off.

Term

It's easy to get tongue-tied with this one. The loan term is one of the terms of the loan. "Loan term" refers to the length of the loan while "terms" indicates the conditions or provisos of the loan. For small investment properties, you can usually obtain a loan with a term comparable to the 30 years you would get on a personal residence. For larger residential properties, the loan term will be shorter—perhaps 20 to 25 years; and for commercial, perhaps shorter yet.

Balloon Loan: A loan in which the periodic payment is based on a long term (typically 15 to 30 years) but where the full outstanding balance comes due in a single payment, the "balloon," much earlier (3 to 10 years).

It is very common for a loan on commercial property to be structured as a "balloon mortgage," which provides a nice compromise between the needs of the lender and those of the borrower. Recall what I said earlier: Principal, rate, term, and payment all interact mathematically. Commercial lenders prefer to have their loan funds committed for relatively short periods of time. With a regular level-payment loan, if the lender requires a shorter term, then the payments must necessarily be larger in order to retire that loan in that amount of time. A balloon loan, however, works like this: The periodic payment (probably a monthly payment) is calculated as if the loan has a relatively long term—say 15 to 30 years. You dutifully make your payments as required, but at the end of a stipulated period, usually 3 to 10 years, the loan "balloons"—that is, the entire remaining balance comes due. You, the borrower, get manageable monthly payments and the lender gets paid off in 3 to 10 years.

Rule of Thumb: Obviously, the "gotcha" is that you must be able to pay off the loan when the balloon comes due. Winning the lottery is always one option. A more conservative plan is to refinance into a new loan when you need to pay the balloon. Your concern, of course, is that there is no guarantee that you'll be able to do so when the time comes. If you find the economy wallowing in the depths of a major recession and credit is unavailable, perhaps you'll be unable to obtain a new loan. 1974 comes to mind, as does the early 1990s. With circumstances really that bad, your lender might very well prefer to negotiate an extension on the balloon rather than become a landlord.

On the other hand, in an environment that resembles a normal credit market, the only real issue standing between you and a suc-

*cessful refinance (assuming you haven't defaulted on the previous
loan) is the value of the property. When you consider purchasing
an investment property, if you have any doubt that 5 to 10 years
hence it will be worth at least as much as you paid for it, then you
shouldn't be buying it in the first place.*

Payment

If you have a mortgage loan on your home, then you're probably familiar
with the standard, amortized loan I described in the section, "principal,"
above. You make a fixed payment each month. Part of it pays the interest
due for use of the lender's money for the previous month; whatever is left
is applied to reduction of the principal. Make these payments for the entire
term of the loan and you will eventually repay the entire amount you borrowed, along with a substantial number of dollars of interest.

Given a particular rate of interest and term of loan, how do you figure
the amount of the payment? You can use a complex mathematical formula
(you won't). You can read my book, *What Every Real Estate Investor Need
to Know* (you must). You can use a table or a software tool (you will).

I provide a table of Mortgage Constants in the Appendix that you can
use for this purpose. Although it sounds like an esoteric concept, a
Mortgage Constant is nothing more than the periodic payment on a loan of
$1 at a given rate and term. Consider Table 5.1.

If you need to find the monthly payment on a $186,000 loan at 7 per-
cent for 30 years, you would look up the factor in this table. You find that
the Mortgage Constant is 0.00665302. The constant is the payment on a
loan of $1, so you multiply the constant by 186,000 to find the payment on
$186,000. The answer is $1237.46.

You can also use the free RealData® Calculator software that I mentioned earlier (download it at realdata.com). Among its functions is a mod-

TABLE 5.1 Monthly Mortgage Payment per $1—Mortgage Constant

Years	6.000%	6.125%	6.250%		6.750%	6.875%	7.000%	7.125%
25	0.00644301	0.00651964	0.00659669	~	0.00690912	0.00698825	0.00706779	0.00714773
26	0.00633677	0.00641422	0.00649211	~	0.00680795	0.00688796	0.00696838	0.00704920
27	0.00623985	0.00631811	0.00639682	~	0.00671601	0.00679687	0.00687815	0.00695984
28	0.00615124	0.00623030	0.00630980	~	0.00663227	0.00671397	0.00679609	0.00687862
29	0.00607005	0.00614988	0.00623018	~	0.00655585	0.00663836	0.00672130	0.00680466
30	0.00599551	0.00607611	0.00615717	~	0.00648598	0.00656929	0.00665302	0.00673719

ule that lets you specify any three of the four basic loan terms (principal, interest rate, term, and payment) to compute the one that's unknown.

You'll hear investors speak of obtaining an interest-only loan. Strictly speaking, that's a misnomer because if you paid only the interest you would never pay back the loan. Of course, it is just the payment that is interest only. The loan is usually for a short period of time, at the end of which the entire principal amount must be paid or converted to an amortizing loan. Earlier, I also mentioned a loan that could be less than interest-only for a time, resulting in the balance of the loan increasing through negative amortization.

As I've been discussing these four basic loan terms, you may have noticed that it is almost impossible to mention one without reference to one or more of the others. They are inextricably connected. If the principal and the term of the loan remain constant but the rate goes up, then the payment must go up also. If the principal and rate stay the same but the term gets longer, then the payment goes down. And so on. Play a bit with the RealData calculator module and you can begin to appreciate how each term is a function of the other three.

Points

If you have ever shopped for a mortgage loan, you have undoubtedly had this experience: You see an ad for a loan at an attractive rate. When you read the microscopically fine print or call for additional information, you learn that the loan includes some number of "points."

Loan points, sometimes called "discount points," are a form of prepaid interest. Each point equals one percent of the face amount of the loan. You pay points to the lender as a trade-off in return for a lower interest rate. Think of it as a way of buying down the rate. Do not confuse loan points with the origination fee that lenders or brokers charge. Although you will hear this fee quoted as the number of points charged, the term is then being used in its generic sense, i.e., an amount equal to 1 percent of the loan. In other words, the origination fee is just that—a fee—and not prepaid interest.

You might see a loan offered at 5.5 percent. Your joy turns to dismay when you discover that you must pay two points to obtain this rate. Do you really have to pay the points? Virtually every lender will offer a sliding scale. Pay one point to lower the rate this much, one-and-a-half points to lower it further, and so on. Different lenders will offer different rate/point mixes.

Points: Prepaid interest you pay up front to a lender to secure a loan at a particular rate. A point equals 1 percent of the face amount of the loan. The more points you pay, the lower the interest rate on the loan.

What's the point of points? From the lender's perspective, it's a question of yield and probabilities adding up to a greater overall profit from its portfolio of loans. From your perspective as the borrower, you want to know whether it makes sense to pay the points to secure a lower rate.

Rule of Thumb: You will be most tempted to pay points in order to lower your loan rate when interest rates are high. That will be probably turn out to be a bad idea. If rates are high now, then there is a good chance you will refinance the loan within a few years to obtain a lower rate. The sooner you refinance, the less likely you are to benefit from the use of points to reduce your original rate.

The calculation to compare loans with different combinations of rate and points can be daunting. However, you can make a simple, albeit crude, estimate that will give you an idea of your break-even period. Consider the loan I mentioned above at 5.5 percent with two points. The lender offers you an option of 6 percent with no points. How many years of saving 0.5 percent per year on the rate will it take to justify paying 2 percent to obtain that saving? This technique—which suggests four years as the break-even point—ignores the time value of money, the differential rate at which the two loans amortize and the fact that mortgage interest is tax-deductible while an investor's points must be written off over the life of the loan. Nonetheless, it will give you a quick, rough estimate of how long it takes to earn back the cost of your points.

Rule of Thumb: An even rougher estimate is this: If you expect to sell the property or refinance the loan in less than five years, you're unlikely to benefit from paying points to reduce the loan rate. Even if you hold the loan longer and don't actually lose money on the points, the benefit might be too small to justify the cost.

Keep these considerations in mind: First, points are themselves a form of investment and breaking even isn't good enough. Second, the real estate that you're financing is an investment property. You are less likely to hold onto it for an extended period than you would your personal residence. Third, as your property increases in value, you may want to refinance it in order to get cash you can use to help buy your next investment. Feeling that you're locked into keeping a property and its original mortgage just because you want to earn back the loan points will prove to be an unprofitable distraction.

Loan Fees

In addition to points, there are many other loan fees you may encounter, and they can vary substantially from one lender to the next. Even though they are not literally among the terms of the loan, they certainly affect the total cost of your financing; you should not take them lightly. I'll divide them into three categories. A few of the individual items merit a sidebar comment, which you'll find below.

Lender/Broker Fees—The first group includes fees you pay directly to the lender or the mortgage broker. The lender and broker certainly have a right to profit from their efforts. What is maddening is the practice of itemizing a whole gaggle of costs with vague and sometimes overlapping meanings. What exactly is a funding fee? How is underwriting different from commitment, and because that's their decision-making process, shouldn't it be part of their cost of doing business?

Loan Origination Fee—This is usually expressed in points (i.e., one point equals one percent of the loan), but unlike the points discussed in the previous section it has no bearing on the interest rate. The origination fee is just a fee and not a form of prepaid interest; paying this fee will not lower your rate.

Administration
Application Fee
Broker's Fee
Commitment Fee
Document Preparation and Review
Funding Fee
    Processing
    Tax Service

Underwriting
    Wire Transfer

Rule of Thumb: You can save a lot of money on antacids by not playing the lender-fee shell game. You might never figure out what some of these items mean or whether they have been priced fairly. So don't get hung up on the individual items. Keep your eye on what matters: the total cost. Compare lenders by comparing the total loan cost of each.

Third-Party Fees—Presumably, these are fees that the lender or broker will collect in order to pay for required services. Sometimes a lender will mark up these services or simply not choose the most cost-efficient or suitable practitioner. Part of your lender-selection process should be to ask if you can select your own licensed appraiser, environmental firm, surveyor, or other inspector.

Appraisal—There are a number of important issues concerning the appraisal of the property. For many larger loans and for commercial loans, the lender may require that you use an appraiser with an advanced designation, called MAI, from the Appraisal Institute. If an MAI is not required, then a report from any licensed appraiser is usually acceptable. Ask if you can choose your own appraiser—not because you're trying to rig the outcome but because you want to avoid some possible mistakes.

The first mistake is overpaying. I confess; I did this myself just a few years ago. I was distracted by other issues and found myself greeting an appraiser chosen by the loan underwriter. He billed more than double the going rate. By the time I had reached that point in the process, I had gone too far to turn back.

The second mistake is to use an appraiser who is not familiar with the area. Yes, I've done this too, but I learned my lesson and resolved never to let it happen again. I had used a mortgage broker from out of state. Apparently he figured Connecticut is a small place and an appraiser from anywhere in the state would be just fine. He might as well have brought someone in from Greenland. I knew I was in trouble when she called and asked for directions to the *city* where the property was located. Presumably, an appraiser should be able to gather sufficient physical and financial data about an income property and enough market data about its location to complete an appraisal anywhere. In reality, if the location is totally unfamiliar, there is just so much time a person will spend getting up to speed to complete an assignment. A local appraiser already knows the rental market and the demographics—knows what's hot and what's not. In the case I described the appraiser was unfamiliar with the rental market and the estimate of property value was well off the mark.

The final mistake to watch out for won't be yours. You're paying for the appraisal, so you have a right to receive a copy. If its conclusions don't seem reasonable, check it for errors. I once tried to refinance an income property I own. The final estimate of value was surprisingly low, so I examined the report carefully. Even though I had provided copies of all the leases and rent histories from tax returns, the property's income was substantially misstated. The room counts on the apartments were wrong, along with other key information about the physical property. The mistakes on this report were the most egregious I had ever seen, but t was not the first time I had encountered factual or even mathematical errors in an appraisal. Scrutinize.

> **Rule of Thumb:** *Your best remedy is not to let any of this happen in the first place. Find a reliable, licensed appraiser who is familiar with the area in which you've chosen to invest; then ask any lender with whom you do business to order its report from that appraiser. In most cases the lender will be glad to agree. If you can provide someone who can actually get the work done, you've made the lender's job easier.*

Credit Report—The lender will pull these reports, but you would be wise to do so yourself before you go loan shopping to see if there any errors. You can go to MyFico.com to get your credit score and report from each of the three major reporting bureaus.

Courier—To send documents back and forth.

Environmental Survey—This might or might not be required. It's one of the more costly items on the list so you should shop this service independently.

Other Inspections—Can include engineering survey or pest inspection. Again, shop the costs on your own.

Flood Certificate—Determines whether the property is in a flood hazard area and requires flood insurance.

Survey—Not routinely required but might be necessary if the transaction involves construction or development as well as acquisition.

Legal and Closing

To repeat earlier advice, find a good real estate attorney and stick with him or her.

Attorney/Settlement Fees

Title Insurance—Keep your title policy where you can find it; if you want to refinance the property in the future, it can usually be updated at less than the cost of a new policy.
Title Search
Recording Fee
Tax and Documentary Stamps

You're not done yet. A mortgage loan can contain still more terms and conditions, so you need to be aware of these:

Due on Sale/Assumability

Most mortgages contain a due-on-sale clause. This clause states that if title to the property is transferred without the lender's prior written consent, then the unpaid balance of the loan must be paid immediately. The primary reason for such a clause is to keep below-market rate loans from being handed down from one owner of the property to the next. If there is no due-on-sale clause or if the note specifically allows such a transfer, then the loan is assumable by a new buyer. Is assumability a good thing? If you as a seller can allow the buyer to assume a loan that is at a below-market rate, then you have a bargaining chip you can trade for a higher price or for some other concession you desire. The flip-side advice to a buyer is this: Don't take for granted that the benefit of assuming a mortgage comes without a price—the seller will probably be looking for a balancing concession.

If you're the seller, have your attorney scrutinize the assumabilty language in your mortgage note. It might be that you will remain liable until the note is paid, even if you have sold the property that was the original security for that note. Seller beware.

Prepayment Penalty and Lockout Period

Prepayment penalties are fairly common in loans on investment real estate. With some commercial loans, you might first encounter what is called a lockout period, during which you cannot retire the loan by sale or refinance. Once that is over, there is a period during which you would be assessed a prepayment penalty, usually in the form of a percentage of the loan balance. Finally, at a later date, the restrictions would expire and you could sell or refinance without penalty.

Recourse

With most loans on investment property, the lender places greater emphasis on the strength of the property than on personal finances of the buyer. Nonetheless, the buyer will still usually be asked to provide a personal guarantee on the loan. This is called a recourse loan because the lender has recourse against the borrower's personal assets in the event of default. If the loan is characterized as nonrecourse, then the lender has no such remedy.

Nonrecourse loans usually prevail with larger commercial properties financed by investment partnerships that have a track record in operating such properties. As a beginning investor, you can rely on the fact that the lender will demand your personal guarantee on a recourse loan.

Impounds

Many lenders will require that you escrow money every month so that it will be available when the property tax and insurance bills come due. If you're the sort of person who could benefit from the discipline imposed by having to set a little aside each month for these significant costs, then this might work to your benefit. If you don't need anyone to help you manage your bills and if you have a choice in the matter, then decline the impound of funds. You might as well have the use of your money until the bills arrive.

Acceleration

With a Beamer, this is a good thing. With a mortgage, it's not. Acceleration is a polite way of saying that you've done something really bad and the lender demands that you cough up the entire unpaid balance at once. You might have failed to make timely payments or you might have allowed the property—which is the security for the loan—to go to ruin. All mortgage notes have acceleration clauses. Examine yours to be sure there are no unreasonable grounds for acceleration and that there *is* a reasonable grace period during which you can repent for your transgression.

Secondary Financing

It is not uncommon for lenders to prohibit secondary financing or at least to reserve the right to approve any subordinate loan. I once obtained a loan where this provision wasn't disclosed in the commitment letter. I discovered it at the closing when I actually read the note. Lesson learned: Don't assume you'll be told everything you need to know. If the lender hasn't specifically provided details in advance on each of the issues above (as in, "There is no penalty for prepayment."), then ask.

6

How Much Can You Borrow?

You may have noticed that your friendly finance company does not simply hand you a blank check and say, "Fill in what you need. You want a toaster with that?" Lenders have a deep and abiding fascination with collateral and with the likelihood of getting repaid. You need to see the process as your lender sees it, and so there are two measurements you must understand before you seek a loan on an income property: Loan-to-Value Ratio and Debt Coverage Ratio. These are underwriting terms; that is, they are part of the lender's decision-making process in granting or not granting your loan request.

Loan-to-Value Ratio (LTV)

The Loan-to-Value Ratio (LTV) establishes the maximum loan amount that the lender will give. It is expressed as a percentage. In general an LTV of 80 percent means the lender is willing to loan up to 80 percent of the property's value.

"Value" and "loan" have particular meanings when you talk about LTV, however, so it's time for a more formal definition:

> **Loan-to-Value Ratio:** *The ratio between the total amount of a property's mortgage financing and the lesser of the property's appraised value or selling price.*

Loan-to-Value = Total Loan Amount / lesser of Appraised Value or Selling
Price

Let's say that you contract to buy a property for $1 million dollars and
you approach a lender that offers 80 percent loan-to-value. If the property's
appraisal comes in at $900,000, then the maximum amount the lender will
consider is 80 percent of the lower figure (the $900,000 appraised value),
or $720,000. On the other hand, if the appraisal comes in at $1.2 million,
you can congratulate yourself on the great deal you negotiated, but don't
expect the lender to join the celebration. Again the loan will hit a limit of
80 percent of the lesser amount, in this case 80 percent of $1 million, or
$800,000.

Clearly, the property appraisal is one of the limiting factors in determining how much you can borrow, so you should be aware of how the professional appraiser goes about this task. The appraiser will base his or her
estimate on three approaches to value: the comparable sales approach, the
cost approach, and the income approach.

If you have ever shopped for a home, then you've certainly used an
informal version of the comparable sales method. You looked at comparable properties that had sold recently in the same or similar locations. Then
you made adjustments to account for how the subject property differed
from the comparables. For example, comp #1 sold for $500,000 but it has
a two-car garage, central air conditioning, and a brand new kitchen. The
subject property has a two-car garage, no central air, and an old-fashioned
kitchen so it should be worth $X less. The appraiser will typically use the
three best comparables available and follow essentially the same reasoning.
This approach is generally best suited to single-family properties.

With the cost approach, the appraiser estimates what it would cost to
build the physical structure today, then depreciates it some amount to
account for the fact that the subject property is not brand new (if that is in
fact the case), and finally adds in the value of the land. As you might suspect, this approach works best with properties that are relatively new.

The last of the approaches, income, is what I discuss in this book and
at length in *What Every Real Estate Investor Needs to Know about Cash
Flow*. With this approach, the appraiser evaluates the property's income
stream and applies a capitalization rate to estimate the value. For smaller-
income properties (two to four units), the appraiser may use a combination

of comparable sales and a simpler income technique, the Gross Rent Multiplier. You might think of this as a "comparable rents approach." If other comparable multifamily homes are selling for seven times their gross rent, then this property should command a similar selling price.

Figure 6.1 shows a sample of the FNMA form that appraisers typically use for small residential income properties.

Multiple mortgage loans present a special issue in regard to the Loan-to-Value calculation. Consider a situation where you own a property with a first mortgage from a bank and a second mortgage from the former owner. You want to refinance the first loan. (For you to do this, the second mortgage holder will have to agree to subordinate to the new loan.) In this case the loan amount in the LTV ratio is not just the first mortgage but rather the sum of all mortgages.

An example will make this clearer. You own a property with an appraised value of $1 million. This is a refinance, so purchase price is not an issue; there is no sale transaction and the appraised value is the only value. The lender offers first-mortgage financing at 80 percent loan to value. 80 percent of $1 million is $800,000.

You intend to refinance your first mortgage but also to keep in place the $200,000 second mortgage loan you obtained from the seller. The $200k counts as part of the "loan" in LTV, so the first-mortgage lender will consider giving you up to $600,000—the difference between the 800,000 justified by LTV and the 200,000 you already have outstanding.

LTV is an underwriting issue; it is one of the ways that the lender measures the degree of risk in providing the loan. 80 percent LTV is another way of saying, "We expect you to have some of your own money on the table here—20 percent of the deal."

Risk is always a consideration for a lender. Even though the loan is secured by a piece of property, the last thing the lender wants to do is take over that property. Being a landlord is not part of their business model. If you're financing a personal residence, you can obtain a loan with less than 20 percent down because there are at least two factors that can reduce the risk: 1) Private Mortgage Insurance (PMI), which insures the portion of the loan that exceeds the usual LTV percentage and 2) the fact that a borrower is less likely to default on a personal residence mortgage than on a loan for an investment property. When you're financing an investment property, the lender sees this as a riskier loan and wants to offset some of that risk. The

FIGURE 6.1   Small Residential Income Property Appraisal Report.

SMALL RESIDENTIAL INCOME PROPERTY APPRAISAL REPORT   File No.

SUBJECT

Property Address		City		State	Zip Code

Legal Description
County

Assessor's Parcel No. | Tax Year | R.E. Taxes $ | Special Assessments $

Neighborhood or Project Name | Map Reference | Census Tract

Borrower | Current Owner | Occupant ☐ Owner ☐ Tenant ☐ Vacant

Property rights appraised ☐ Fee Simple ☐ Leasehold   Project Type ☐ PUD ☐ Condominium   HOA$ /Mo.

Sales Price $ | Date of Sale | Description and $ amount of loan charges/concessions to be paid by seller

Lender/Client | Address

Appraiser | Address

NEIGHBORHOOD

Location	☐ Urban ☐ Suburban ☐ Rural	Predominant Single Family Occupancy	Single family housing PRICE $ (000) AGE (yrs)	Predominant 2-4 Family Occupancy	2-4 family housing PRICE $ (000) AGE (yrs)
Built up	☐ Over 75% ☐ 25-75% ☐ Under 25%	☐ Owner		☐ Owner	
Growth rate	☐ Rapid ☐ Stable ☐ Slow	☐ Tenant	Low	☐ Tenant	Low
Property values	☐ Increasing ☐ Stable ☐ Declining	☐ Vacant (0-5%)	High	☐ Vacant (0-5%)	High
Demand/supply	☐ Shortage ☐ In balance ☐ Over supply	☐ Vacant (over 5%)	Predominant	☐ Vacant (over 5%)	Predominant
Marketing time	☐ Under 3 mos. ☐ 3-6 mos. ☐ Over 6 mos.				

Typical 2-4 family bldg. Type _____   No. stories _____ No. units _____ Age _____ yrs

Typical rents $ _____ to $ _____   ☐ Increasing ☐ Stable ☐ Declining

Est. neighborhood apt. vacancy _____ %   ☐ Increasing ☐ Stable ☐ Declining

Rent controls ☐ Yes ☐ No ☐ Likely   If yes or likely, describe _____

Present land use %   One family _____   2-4 family _____   Multi-family _____   Commercial _____   (_____)

Land use change ☐ Not likely ☐ Likely ☐ In process to:

Note: Race and the racial composition of the neighborhood are not appraisal factors.

Neighborhood boundaries and characteristics: _____

Factors that affect the marketability of the properties in the neighborhood (proximity to employment and amenities, employment stability, appeal to market, etc.): _____

The following available listings represent the most current, similar, and proximate competitive properties to the subject property in the subject neighborhood. This analysis is intended to evaluate the inventory currently on the market competing with the subject property in the subject neighborhood and recent price and marketing time trends affecting the subject property. (Listings outside the subject neighborhood are not considered applicable). The listing comparables can be the rental or sale comparables if they are currently for sale.

ITEM	SUBJECT	COMPARABLE LISTING NO. 1	COMPARABLE LISTING NO. 2	COMPARABLE LISTING NO. 3
Address				
Proximity to subject				
Listing price	$	☐ Unf. ☐ Furn. $	☐ Unf. ☐ Furn. $	☐ Unf. ☐ Furn. $
Approximate GBA				
Data source				
# Units/Tot. rms./BR/BA				
Approximate year built				
Approx. days on market				

Comparison of listings to subject property: _____

Market conditions that affect 2-4 family properties in the subject neighborhood (including the above neighborhood indicators of growth rate, property values, demand/supply, and marketing time) and the prevalence and impact in the subject market area regarding loan discounts, interest buydowns and concessions, and identification of trends in listing prices, average days on market and any change over past year, etc.: _____

SITE

Dimensions _____   Topography _____

Site area _____   Corner lot ☐ No ☐ Yes   Size _____

Specific zoning classification and description _____   Shape _____

Zoning compliance ☐ Legal ☐ Legal nonconforming (Grandfathered use) ☐ Illegal ☐ No zoning   Drainage _____

Highest & best use as improved: ☐ Present use ☐ Other use (explain) _____   View _____   Landscaping _____

Utilities	Public	Other	Off-site Improvements Type	Public	Private	
Electricity			Street			Driveway _____
Gas			Curb/gutter			Apparent easements _____
Water			Sidewalk			FEMA Special Flood Hazard Area ☐ Yes ☐ No
Sanitary sewer			Street lights			FEMA Zone _____ Map Date _____
Storm sewer			Alley			FEMA Map No. _____

COMMENTS

Comments (apparent adverse easements, encroachments, special assessments, slide areas, illegal or legal nonconforming zoning, use, etc.): _____

SMALL RESIDENTIAL INCOME PROPERTY APPRAISAL REPORT

General description	Exterior description (Materials/condition)	Foundation	Insulation (R-value if known)
Units/bldg. _____ /	Foundation _____	Slab _____	☐ Roof
Stories _____	Exterior walls _____	Crawl space _____	☐ Ceiling
Type (det./att) _____	Roof surface _____	Sump Pump _____	☐ Walls
Design (style) _____	Gutters & dwnspts. _____	Dampness _____	☐ Floor
Existing/proposed _____	Window type _____	Settlement _____	☐ None
Under construction _____	Storm sash/Screens _____	Infestation _____	Adequacy _____
Year Built _____	Manufactured housing* ☐ Yes ☐ No	Basement _____	Energy efficient items: _____
Effective age(yrs.) _____	* (Complies with the HUD Manufactured Housing Construction and Safety Standards)	Basement finish _____ % of 1st floor area	

DESCRIPTION

Units	Level(s)	Foyer	Living	Dining	Kitchen	Den	Family rm.	Bedrooms	# Baths	Laundry	Other	Sq. ft./unit	Total ☑

Improvements contain: _____ Rooms; _____ Bedroom(s); _____ Bath(s); _____ Square feet of GROSS BUILDING AREA

GROSS BUILDING AREA (GBA) IS DEFINED AS THE TOTAL FINISHED AREA (INCLUDING COMMON AREAS) OF THE IMPROVEMENTS BASED UPON EXTERIOR MEASUREMENTS.

OF IMPROVEMENTS

Surfaces (Materials/condition)	Heating	Kitchen equip. (# / unit- cond.)	Attic	Car Storage No. Cars _____
Floors _____	Type _____	Refrigerator _____	☐ None	Garage
Walls _____	Fuel _____	Range/oven _____	☐ Stairs	Carport
Trim/finish _____	Condition _____	Disposal _____	☐ Drop stair	Attached
Bath floor _____		Dishwasher _____	☐ Scuttle	Detached
Bath wainscot _____	Cooling	Fan/hood _____	☐ Floor	Adequate
Doors _____	Central _____	Compactor _____	☐ Heated	Inadequate
	Other _____	Washer/dryer _____	☐ Finished	Offstreet
	Condition _____	Microwave _____	☐ Unfinished	None
Fireplace(s) # _____		Intercom _____		

Condition of the improvements, repairs needed, quality of construction, additional features, modernization, etc.: _____

Depreciation (physical, functional, and external inadequacies, etc.): _____

ADDITIONAL COMMENTS

Adverse environmental conditions (such as, but not limited to, hazardous wastes, toxic substances, etc.) present in the improvements, on the site, or in the immediate vicinity of the subject property: _____

VALUATION ANALYSIS

COST APPROACH

ESTIMATED SITE VALUE .... = $ _____

ESTIMATED REPRODUCTION COST---NEW OF IMPROVEMENTS:

_____ Sq. Ft. @ $ _____	= $ 0.00
_____ Sq. Ft. @ $ _____	= $ 0.00
_____ Sq. Ft. @ $ _____	= $ 0.00
_____ Sq. Ft. @ $ _____	= $ 0.00
_____ Sq. Ft. @ $ _____	= $ 0.00
_____	= $ _____
_____	= $ _____
_____	= $ _____
_____	= $ _____

Special Energy Efficient Items _____ = $ _____

Porches, Patios, etc _____ = $ _____

Total Estimated Cost New .... = $ _____

	Physical	Functional	External
Less Depreciation			= $ _____

Depreciated Value of Improvements .... = $ _____

"As is" Value of Site Improvements .... = $ _____

INDICATED VALUE BY COST APPROACH .... = $ _____

Comments on Cost Approach (such as, source of cost estimate, site value, square foot calculation and, for HUD and VA, the estimated remaining economic life of the property): _____

FIGURE 6.1   Small Residential Income Property Appraisal Report.

81

At least three rental comparables should be reported and analyzed in this section. The rental comparables should represent the most current rental information on properties as similar and proximate to the subject property as possible. (This comparison is based on current rental data, therefore, the rental comparables typically are not the same comparables used in the sales comparison analysis.) The appraisal report should assure the reader that the units and properties selected as comparables are comparable to the subject property (both the units and the overall property) and accurately represent the rental market for the subject property (unless otherwise stated within the report).

ITEM	SUBJECT	COMPARABLE RENTAL NO. 1	COMPARABLE RENTAL NO. 2	COMPARABLE RENTAL NO. 3
Address				
Proximity to subject				
Lease data (if available)				
Rent survey date				
Data source				
Rent concessions				

Description of property—units, design, appeal, age, vacancies, and conditions	No. Units No. Vac. Yr. Blt.	No. Units No. Vac. Yr. Blt.:	No. Units No. Vac. Yr. Blt.:	No. Units No. Vac. Yr. Blt.:

Individual unit breakdown

	Rm. Count (Tot, Br, Ba)	Size Sq. Ft.	Rm. Count (Tot, Br, Ba)	Size Sq. Ft.	Total Monthly Rent	Rm. Count (Tot, Br, Ba)	Size Sq. Ft.	Total Monthly Rent	Rm. Count (Tot, Br, Ba)	Size Sq. Ft.	Total Monthly Rent

Utilities, furniture, and amenities included in rent

Functional utility, basement, heating/cooling, project amenities, etc

Analysis of rental data and support for estimated market rents for the individual subject units (including the adjustments used, the adequacy of comparables, rental concessions, etc.)

Subject's rent schedule   The rent schedule reconciles the applicable indicated monthly market rents to the appropriate subject unit, and provides the estimated rents for the subject property. The appraiser must review the rent characteristics of the comparable sales to determine whether estimated rents should reflect actual or market rents. For example, if actual rents were available on the sales comparables and used to derive the gross rent multiplier (GRM), actual rents for the subject should be used. If market rents were used to construct the comparables' rents and derive the GRM, market rents should be used. The total gross estimated rent must represent rent characteristics consistent with the sales comparable data used to derive the GRM. The total gross estimated rent is not adjusted for vacancy.

Unit	LEASES — Lease Date (Begin)	Lease Date (End)	No. Units Vacant	ACTUAL RENTS — Per Unit (Unfurnished)	Per Unit (Furnished)	Total Rents	ESTIMATED RENTS — Per Unit (Unfurnished)	Per Unit (Furnished)	Total Rents
				$	$	$	$	$	$
						$			$

Other monthly income (itemize) .... $ ....

Vacancy: Actual last year _____ % Previous year _____ % Estimated: _____ % $ _____ Annually   Total gross estimated rent $ ....

Utilities included in estimated rents: ☐ Electric ☐ Water ☐ Sewer ☐ Gas ☐ Oil ☐ Trash collection ☐

Comments on the rent schedule, actual rents, estimated rents (especially regarding differences between actual and estimated rents), utilities, etc.:

FIGURE 6.1   Small Residential Income Property Appraisal Report.

SMALL RESIDENTIAL INCOME PROPERTY APPRAISAL REPORT

The undersigned has recited three recent sales of properties most similar and proximate to the subject property and has described and analyzed these in this analysis. If there is a significant variation between the subject and comparable properties, the analysis includes a dollar adjustment reflecting the market reaction to those items or an explanation supported by the market data. If a significant item in the comparable property is superior to, or more favorable than, the subject property, a minus (-) adjustment is made, thus reducing the adjusted sales price of the comparable property; if a significant item in the comparable property is inferior to, or less favorable than, the subject property, a plus (+) adjustment is made, thus increasing the adjusted sales price of the comparable property. [(1) Sales Price ÷ Gross Monthly Rent]

ITEM	SUBJECT	COMPARABLE SALE NO. 1	COMPARABLE SALE NO. 2	COMPARABLE SALE NO. 3
Address				
Proximity to subject				
Sales price	$	☐ Unf. ☐ Furn. $	☐ Unf. ☐ Furn. $	☐ Unf. ☐ Furn. $
Sales price per GBA	$	$	$	$
Gross monthly rent	$	$	$	$
Gross mo. rent mult. (1)				
Sales price per unit	$	$	$	$
Sales price per room	$	$	$	$
Data and/or Verification Sources				

ADJUSTMENTS	DESCRIPTION	DESCRIPTION	+(-)$ Adjustment	DESCRIPTION	+(-)$ Adjustment	DESCRIPTION	+(-)$ Adjustment
Sales or financing concessions							
Date of sale/time							
Location							
Leasehold/Fee Simple							
Site							
View							
Design and appeal							
Quality of construction							
Age							
Condition							
Gross Building Area	Sq. ft.	Sq. ft.		Sq. ft.		Sq. ft.	
Unit breakdown	No. of units / Rm. count Tot Br Ba / No. Vac.						
Basement description							
Functional utility							
Heating/cooling							
Parking on/off site							
Project amenities and fee (if applicable)							
Net Adj. (total)		☐ + ☐ - $		☐ + ☐ - $		☐ + ☐ - $	
Adjusted sales price of comparable		$		$		$	

Comments on sales comparison (including reconciliation of all indicators of value as to consistency and relative strength and evaluation of the typical investor's/purchaser's motivation in that market): _____

ITEM	SUBJECT	COMPARABLE NO. 1	COMPARABLE NO. 2	COMPARABLE NO. 3
Date, Price and Data Source for prior sales within year of appraisal				

Analysis of any current agreement of sale, option, or listing of the subject property and analysis of any prior sales of subject and comparables within one year of the date of appraisal.

Total gross monthly estimated rent $ _____ x gross rent multiplier (GRM) _____ = $ _____ INDICATED VALUE BY INCOME APPROACH

Comments on income approach (including expense ratios, if available, and reconciliation of the GRM) _____

INDICATED VALUE BY SALES COMPARISON APPROACH . . . . $ ____

INDICATED VALUE BY INCOME APPROACH . . . . $ ____

INDICATED VALUE BY COST APPROACH . . . . $ ____

This appraisal is made ☐ "as is" ☐ subject to the repairs, alterations, inspections, or conditions listed below ☐ subject to completion per plans and specifications.

Comments and conditions of appraisal: _____

Final reconciliation: _____

The purpose of this appraisal is to estimate the market value of the real property that is the subject of this report, based on the above conditions and the certification, contingent and limiting conditions, and market value definition that are stated in the attached Freddie Mac Form 439/Fannie Mae Form 1004B (Revised _____).

I (WE) ESTIMATE THE MARKET VALUE, AS DEFINED, OF THE REAL PROPERTY THAT IS THE SUBJECT OF THIS REPORT, AS OF _____ (WHICH IS THE DATE OF INSPECTION AND THE EFFECTIVE DATE OF THIS REPORT) TO BE $ _____

APPRAISER:	SUPERVISORY APPRAISER (ONLY IF REQUIRED):	
Signature	Signature	☐ Did ☐ Did Not
Name	Name	Inspect Property
Date Report Signed	Date Report Signed	
State Certification # _____ State	State Certification # _____ State	
Or State License # _____ State	Or State License # _____ State	

Freddie Mac Form 72 10-94   10 CH.   PAGE 4 OF 4   Fannie Mae Form 1025 10-94

FIGURE 6.1 Small Residential Income Property Appraisal Report.

83

best way to do so is to require the borrower to have real money invested in the deal. The more equity (i.e., down payment), the less likely you are to walk away from the property and give it back to the bank if you hit a rough spot in your cash flow. In addition, the smaller the loan in relation to the value of the property, the greater the lender's chances of recovering all that is owed in the event of a foreclosure.

> **Rule of Thumb:** *The required Loan-to-Value Ratio for investment property will typically range from 60 percent to 80 percent, depending on the type of property, its size, and its location. You might at times encounter an LTV as low as 50 percent or as high as 90 percent. Apartment buildings tend toward 80 percent and occasionally higher, while other types of investment property will usually be lower. The ratio will also depend, of course, on the particular lender, so it is essential that you survey the mortgage market to find the loan that suits your needs.*

Debt Coverage Ratio (DCR)

When you finance the purchase of a home, the lender will examine two ratios: your housing or "front-end" ratio and your debt or "back-end" ratio. The first compares your total monthly mortgage payment to your monthly income; the latter compares all of your monthly obligations, including mortgage, to your monthly income. In order to qualify for a loan with a particular lender, each ratio must be no more than a certain percentage—usually around 28 percent for housing and perhaps 36 percent to 40 percent—but sometimes as high as the mid-40s—for debt. The rationale is that you must demonstrate sufficient income to be able to service the mortgage debt.

Here, specifically, is how this type of qualification works. The loan underwriter calculates your front-end ratio by taking your proposed "PITI" housing expense—that's the monthly payment for principal, interest, taxes, and property insurance—and divides it by your total monthly pretax income. The underwriter then computes your back-end ratio by combining that same PITI housing expense along with all other monthly debt payments and again dividing by your pretax monthly income. Debt payments will of course include car payments and other loans. Most underwriters will use the minimum required monthly payment as your credit card debt.

Example

You're contemplating the purchase of a four-family property. You will live in one unit, and the other three rentals provide a total monthly gross of $3600, of which the lender will count 75 percent as income. The purchase price is $370,000 and you are looking for a mortgage with 80 percent loan-to-value at 7.25 percent for 25 years. Monthly property taxes will be $360 and monthly insurance $180. Your monthly employment income is $7200. You also have a car payment of $275 and monthly credit card minimum payments of $230. The lender's qualify ratios are 28 percent front-end and 36 percent back-end. Based on this information and assuming your credit rating is satisfactory, will you qualify for the loan?

First, calculate the amount of the loan:

$370,000 × 80% = $296,000

Next, go to the Appendix and use the table of Mortgage Constants to calculate the monthly principal and interest payment on a loan of this size at 7.25 percent for 25 years:

0.00722807 × $296,000 = $2,139.51

Now calculate your front-end ratio:

Principal and Interest + Taxes + Insurance / Monthly Income
($2,139.51 + $360 + $180) / ($7,200 + ($3,600 x 75%))
$2,679.51 / $9,990 = 26.82%

You're under the 28-percent limit on the front-end ratio. Now calculate the back-end:

Principal and Interest + Taxes + Insurance + Other Debt / Monthly Income
($2,139.51 + $360 + $180 + $275 + $230) / ($7,200 + ($3,600 x 75%))
$3,184.51 / $9,990 = 31.88%

You're comfortably under the maximum back-end ratio. You've met both tests, so your income is sufficient to qualify.

The financing of an investment property follows similar reasoning, but now the lender is typically more interested in the property's income than in yours. In other words, does the *property* produce enough cash to service the debt?

Debt Coverage Ratio (also called Debt Service Coverage Ratio):
The ratio between a property's Net Operating Income (NOI) and its
Annual Debt Service (ADS).

DCR = Net Operating Income / Annual Debt Service

Elsewhere in this book and throughout *What Every Real Estate Investor Needs to Know about Cash Flow,* I've emphasized the importance of Net Operating Income as a benchmark figure for any income property. It manifests its importance again as you consider financing. Recall how it's calculated:

Gross Scheduled Income
Less Vacancy and Credit Loss
= Gross Operating Income

_____

less Operating Expenses
= Net Operating Income

NOI is the property's net income *before* the impact of financing or income taxes. Another way of looking at NOI is that it's the amount you have available to cover debt service and taxes and to provide you with cash flow. It should be clear why NOI is important to the lender. If it's the money you have available for debt service, is it enough?

When you have exactly enough NOI to make the mortgage payments, then your Debt Coverage Ratio is 1.00—the NOI and ADS are the same, so NOI / ADS = 1.00. Here's something you can take to the bank: 1.00 isn't good enough. Not ever. It means you expect to have just enough net income to make your loan payments. From your lender's point of view, just enough is not good enough. Any cash flow surprise—any loss of income or unanticipated expense—will mean you lack the funds you need to make payments on the loan. Your lender will require a cushion as part of the process of qualifying your property for the loan and that cushion will be at least 20 percent.

Example

You have four apartments that rent for $1000 per month each. You allow for a 2-percent vacancy and credit loss. Your annual operating expenses are $19,100. You bought the property with a $250,000 mortgage loan at 7-percent annual interest for 240 months. You consult the mortgage payment tables at the back of this book to determine that the monthly payment for this loan is $1938.25. What is the property's Debt Coverage Ratio?

Using the model above, you can plug in the numbers as follows:

4 apartments x $1,000 $\times$ 12 = $48,000 Gross Scheduled Income

 Less 2% Vacancy and Credit Allowance, $960

 Less $19,100 Operating Expenses

equals $27,940 Net Operating Income

$1,938.25 Monthly Mortgage Payment times 12 equals $23,259 Annual Debt Service

$27,940 Net Operating Income divided by $23,259 Annual Debt Service equals 1.20 Debt Coverage Ratio

Rule of Thumb: *You should expect that a cushion of 20 percent—a Debt Coverage Ratio of 1.20— is the least that your lender will require. (Side-note to sticklers: Yes, I have seen a rare 1.15 DCR with apartments or senior housing. Of course, I also thought I saw a purple cow once, so this report might be unreliable.) 1.20 is by no means the highest DCR you might encounter. Ratios for hotel, restaurant, and special-purpose properties are routinely higher; ratios for any type of investment property can reach 1.50 to 2.00 or even more in a given market.*

As you've seen earlier in our discussion, there is a basic principle of math that if you know all of the variables in an equation except one, you can calculate the value of that missing piece. In looking at Debt Coverage Ratio so far, the missing piece has been the ratio itself. In other words, you've known the mortgage terms (and therefore the Annual Debt Service) as well as the NOI; with that information you've been able to compute the DCR to see if it was acceptable. You may want to approach this from a different angle, however. Once you have surveyed your lenders and determined the minimum acceptable DCR for each, it would be reasonable to ask, "If I know the Net Operating Income, the loan terms and the Debt Coverage Ratio, what is the maximum loan that I could expect?"

For those of you with altogether too much free time, the calculation can be done manually. The formula is as follows:

Maximum Loan Amount = Net Operating Income / Debt Coverage Ratio /
(Monthly Mortgage Constant × 12)

where the monthly mortgage constant equals the monthly payment for a $1
mortgage at a given interest rate and term.

Thanks to modern technology, you don't have to go to all that trouble.
If you haven't heeded my urging already, download the RealData®
Calculator from www.realdata.com. Another of its functions is "Maximum
Loan Supported by Property Income." Say that you find a lender offering a
15-year loan at 7.375 percent. Your property's Net Operating Income is
$80,000 and the lender requires a Debt Coverage Ratio of at least 1.25.
Make those entries and the answer appears in a flash (see Figure 6.2).

Maximum Loan Supported by Property Income

Net Operating Income	$80,000.00
Lender's Debt Coverage Ratio	1.2500
Term of Loan in Months	180
Loan Interest Rate (annual)	7.3750%
Maximum Loan Supported by NOI	$579,758.47

FIGURE 6.2   Screen shot from the RealData® Calculator, available at
www.realdata.com.

The property's income can justify a loan of about $580,000.

All Cash, No Cash, or Some Borrowed Money?

Whether it's a great deal, an OK deal, or a terrible deal, a real estate invest-ment is almost certainly going to have a significant price tag attached. Once you have found a promising property to buy, one of the very first questions you will ask yourself is, "How am I going to pay for this?" Logically, you have three choices: You can pay the entire cost with your own money; you can pay entirely with other people's money; or you can mix and match, using some cash and some financing.

Right now you're probably expecting me to say that there is one uni-versally correct answer to this question and then to pull that little bunny right out of a hat. Sorry, but nothing worth knowing or doing is ever quite that simple. If it were, everyone on the planet would be making successful real estate deals and I wouldn't have to write this book.

I am going to tell you, eventually, that I think one of the three is likely to be the best choice much of the time, but the reality is that the other dogs can also have their days (if I may mix my animal metaphors). We're going to look at this topic in considerable detail not only for its own sake, but also because it brings into focus a key principle of real estate investment, one that you must never lose sight of: Investing is all about the numbers; it's about understanding the expected future income stream. In order for you to have a grasp of what you're getting into, especially if you are a beginning investor, you have to run the numbers on every deal.

All Cash

Let's say you have identified an investment property that you can and would like to purchase for $200,000. Lucky you—you just happen to have $200,000 in folding green cash available to close this deal. Should you use that cash? The answer is a resounding maybe.

Because you're interested in real estate investing, you have undoubtedly heard the term "leverage." I'll discuss that in more detail in a moment, but for now just think back to your high-school physics class and to the picture of a 97-pound weakling using a lever to move a big rock. Financial leverage operates on the same model. You employ minimal resources to accomplish an amplified result. If you use your own cash to pay for an investment property in its entirety, then you are using zero leverage. You are not amplifying your resources. You're walking up to that rock, hoisting it on your shoulder all by yourself and walking home with it.

That sounds like something you'll never want to do. Actually, there are a few occasions when it might make excellent sense. One such occasion is when you are in a position to use a different kind of lever: cash as a negotiating tool. I did exactly this on a deal some years ago. The seller thought she had her property sold. The deal dragged on and on and the buyer ultimately failed to obtain the financing he needed to complete the purchase. The seller was frustrated and annoyed and more than a little skeptical of the next yo-yo who might come along and offer to purchase the property subject to obtaining a mortgage loan. I offered to purchase the property for all cash and to close just as soon as our lawyers could fire up their typewriters. But I would purchase only if she reduced the price significantly. What would she prefer? A certain and immediate sale at a discount or an encore of the previous unsatisfying performance? Deal done.

> **Rule of Thumb:** Keep in mind that buying a property for all cash doesn't mean your bank is going to excommunicate you. If you have access to the cash and can use it to negotiate a better all-cash pur-

chase price, you can do that and still go to the bank later for a mortgage loan that will replenish your funds. In fact, depending on the timing of the transaction and the efficiency with which you and your lender can operate, you might have financing in place in time to use the lender's money at the closing. This is not an issue for the seller (and not something to which the seller can properly object), because as long as you have promised to pay in cash and have not placed any mortgage contingency in the purchase contract, you can come to the closing and pay with a lender's cash as well as your own.

Another time you might want to purchase a property for all cash is when your horizon for reselling the property is short. This book is about investing, not about "flipping" properties. Nonetheless, there may be times when you expect that you will not own the property for very long. For example, you might see that the property has obvious deficiencies in its management—perhaps it has rents that are significantly below market—deficiencies that you can remedy within a year or two. If you enhance a property's income stream, then you immediately create value.

I once purchased a property that was absolutely exquisite and in excellent physical condition. The seller had owned it for many years and was out of touch with the kind of rental income it could command. I purchased it; within three years, during the recession of the mid-70s, I rolled over all the leases at market rates and sold the building for twice the original price.

What does this story have to do with buying for all cash? Procuring a loan for an income property involves costs and fees. Sometimes they might be minimal, especially with small residential properties, but often they may involve surveys, environmental studies, professional appraisals, and a variety of lender fees. If you keep the property (and the loan) for a period of years, then the impact of these nonrecurring costs—which you can look at as part of the cost of your investment—will be spread out over time and should have a relatively small impact on the return you experience on your investment. On the other hand, if your purchase is loaded with a lot of loan-related costs and then you turn the property over quickly, these costs will drag down your overall return.

Once again, keep in mind that you can always go back to the well. You might purchase a property for all cash, expecting to turn the property over quickly. If you see that's not going to happen, there is nothing to prevent you from going to the bank and pulling your cash back out via a mortgage loan.

> **Rule of Thumb:** *If neither of the reasons discussed above is relevant—if you cannot achieve an advantage negotiating the purchase price by buying for all cash, and if you do not realistically expect to resell the property so soon as to make the paying of loan fees unwarranted—then it is unlikely that you will benefit from making an all-cash purchase.*

No Cash

Thanks to the Internet and spam email, you now hear some variation of this theme every day: *Get Rich Overnight—No Money Down—Get Paid to Eat* (no, I didn't make that up). At every turn, some huckster wants you to believe that you can get something for nothing.

Can you buy income-producing real estate with no money down? *Should* you buy income-producing real estate with no money down? Again the clarion answer is… well, maybe sometimes.

Buying a property with no money down can be done, but there are some realities you must confront if you want to make such a transaction. Unlike the all-cash model I discussed above, a no-cash proposal will not enhance your bargaining position. Quite the contrary, it may cause the seller to wonder, with ample reason, if you have the resources to go through with the purchase. You should look at the negotiation this way: When the seller agrees to tie up a property in a contract with a buyer who is using no cash, the seller feels that he or she has made a concession. Negotiating is all about give and take, trading concessions. You, the buyer, have now used up one of your bargaining chips; you'll probably need to make some sort of concession in return.

> **Rule of Thumb:** *This rule of thumb comes straight from the "If it sounds too good to be true" department. The discussion above assumes that you, the buyer, are the party who is lobbying for a no-cash deal. But what if you find a seller who is advertising "No Money Down" or "Incredible Seller Financing?" My advice is to*

hide under your bed and don't come out until he goes away. It could be a sophisticated seller looking to relieve a capital gain problem by seeking an installment sale, but it's more likely to be a bottom-fisher hoping to unload a problem property by hooking a wannabe investor who is under the spell of get-rich-quick gurus. Sorry if this sounds like tough love, but beware.

The property's future cash flow represents a second area of concern. When a bank loans money on an income property, it looks at that property's ability to generate enough rental income to cover its operating expenses and mortgage payments with room to spare. Specifically, it looks at the Debt Coverage Ratio, which I discussed earlier. This is the ratio of your Net Operating Income to your Annual Debt Service.

Gross Scheduled Income
    Less Vacancy and Credit Allowance
    Less Operating Expenses
    equals Net Operating Income

Monthly Mortgage Payment times 12 equals Annual Debt Service

Net Operating Income divided by Annual Debt Service equals Debt Coverage Ratio

I discussed debt coverage earlier, but it's important enough to review. To translate it from math-speak into plainer English, if your annual net income before mortgage payments exactly equals your total annual mortgage payments, then your Debt Coverage Ratio is 1.00. A DCR of 1.00 means you have just enough money to cover your mortgage payments—not a penny more. If your DCR is greater than 1.00 it means you expect to have more than enough; you have a cushion. Banks, being prudent and cautious institutions, not usually good-natured about losing large sums of money, typically expect your property to have a DCR of 1.20 or greater before they will loan money against it. 1.20 represents a cushion of 20 percent. For some type of properties, the lender might require 1.30 or even more.

With a sound investment property, you should usually find a DCR of 1.20 to be an achievable goal when you finance 70 percent to 80 percent of the purchase price. The wheels may start to come off, however, when you try to finance 100 percent.

Problem 1: You have more debt to repay, so you can expect your total debt service to be greater.

Problem 2: A lender who is providing you with the money to use as the down payment on a property is making a risky loan. Let's say that you're buying a property for $100,000; you plan to get a first mortgage loan from a bank for $80,000 and a $20,000 loan from another source (perhaps the seller). That second loan must line up behind the first mortgage. If you get tired of being a landlord and skip off to Fiji, the first mortgagee (the bank) gets first crack at recovering what is owed to it. Only if there is anything left will the second mortgagee have a chance to collect some part of its debt.

Why would a lender take the risk of loaning you the down payment money? If you're dealing with a third-party lender, you might expect to pay several points and a variety of fees to obtain the loan, as well as an interest rate significantly higher than that of the first mortgage. Your second loan represents a higher risk, so you must pay a higher cost. Now your cash flow feels the double whammy: Not only do you have more debt to pay, but part of the debt will be at a higher rate, thus depleting your cash flow even further.

Problem 3: But wait—there's more. Remember the Debt Coverage Ratio? With one mortgage you might be able to cover your total debt service with room to spare. But now you're paying dearly for this secondary financing. The fact that you have more debt in and of itself increases your total debt payments and thus decreases your Debt Coverage Ratio.

Example

The property you want to purchase has a Net Operating Income of $11,000. You make the optimistic and altogether improbable assumption that the bank will lend you the entire $100,000 at 7 percent for 240 months. What is your Debt Coverage Ratio? Is the bank likely to be happy about this?

Again, using the mortgage payment tables, you determine that the monthly payment on this loan will be $775.30.

$775.30 Monthly Mortgage Payment times 12 equals $9,303.60 Annual Debt Service

$11,000 Net Operating Income divided by $9,303.60 Annual Debt Service equals 1.18 Debt Coverage Ratio

This DCR is borderline at best. Considering that you want to finance 100 percent of the purchase and commit none of your own money, you will need to do significant lobbying to get this loan. If you use a second loan, it is likely to carry a higher rate and a shorter term, making its payments even higher.

Example

Suppose that the bank will loan you a maximum of 80 percent of the purchase price ($80,000) at 7 percent for 240 months, and the best terms you can obtain for a second loan of $20,000 are 11 percent for 84 months. What are your Debt Coverage Ratios with and without the second loan?

First, determine the payment amount for each of the loans. You can use the Mortgage Constant Tables in the back of the book. The monthly constant for a 20-year (240-month) loan at 7 percent is 0.00775299. Do the math:

80,000 × 0.00775299 = 620.24

$80,000 at 7 percent for 240 months requires a monthly payment of $620.24.

The monthly constant for a 7-year (84-month) loan at 11 percent is 0.01712244.

20,000 × 0.01712244 = 342.45

$20,000 at 11 percent for 84 months requires a monthly payment of $342.45.

$620.24 Monthly Mortgage Payment times 12 equals $7,442.88 Annual Debt Service

$342.45 Monthly Mortgage Payment times 12 equals $4,109.40 Annual Debt Service

Total (Combined) Annual Debt Service equals $11,552.28

$11,000 Net Operating Income divided by $7,442.88 Annual Debt Service for first Mortgage equals 1.48 Debt Coverage Ratio

If you use $20,000 of your own money as the down payment and seek just an $80,000 first mortgage, then you'll present the bank with a strong 1.48 Debt Coverage Ratio. What happens when you pile on the second mortgage loan?

$11,000 Net Operating Income divided by $11,552.28 Annual Debt Service equals 0.95 Debt Coverage Ratio

Now your Debt Coverage Ratio has fallen off the bank's radar and you can't expect to obtain the first mortgage loan you were planning on. In fact, a DCR of less than 1.00 means the property doesn't have enough Net Operating Income to cover the loan payments. You would have to support the property, putting in your own cash each month to make up the shortfall.

If you don't have the $20,000 down payment and the bank won't make the loan, where will you go to finance this purchase? Perhaps you will have to go to a lender that will agree to a riskier first mortgage loan—at a price, of course. This no-cash deal is getting awfully expensive.

Example

You find a lender that will loan you 100 percent of the purchase price at 11-percent interest for 180 months. You'll have to pay 4 points ($4000) as a premium to obtain the loan. Are you feeling good about this?

A loan of $100,000 at 11 percent for 180 months requires a monthly payment of $1136.60.

$1,136.60 Monthly Mortgage Payment times 12 equals $13,639.20 Annual Debt Service

If the lender is willing to give you this loan, obviously he or she doesn't care about the Debt Coverage Ratio. You don't even need to do the math to see that the result will be less than 1.00. If you have $11,000 in Net Operating but have to pay $13,639 in debt service, you obviously need to throw in $2639 of your own money to bring your cash flow up to zero. Add to this the fact that it will cost you $4000 in points for this privilege and the answer is no, you're not feeling good about this.

Problem 4: "But wait," you say. "I can get the down payment loan from the seller on very attractive terms." This is such a common practice that it even has a name: Purchase Money Mortgage. This might actually work. You need to run the numbers to know for sure, but for the first time in our discussion of no-cash deals, you do see a glimmer of hope.

Example

You have the same $80,000 loan from the bank as above. The seller offers $20,000 at 6 percent for 240 months but includes an obligation (called a "balloon") that you pay off the outstanding balance no later than month 120. You have no problem with the balloon because you don't expect to keep the property more than 10 years; you can pay the balloon off with the proceeds of the future resale.

The first mortgage loan, as before, requires a monthly payment of $620.24. The Purchase Money Mortgage (PMM) requires $143.29.

$620.24 Monthly Mortgage Payment times 12 equals $7,442.88 Annual Debt Service

$143.29 Monthly PMM Payment times 12 equals $1,719.48 Annual Debt Service

Total (Combined) Annual Debt Service equals $9,162.36

$11,000 Net Operating Income divided by $9,162.36 Annual Debt Service for first mortgage equals 1.20 Debt Coverage Ratio

This looks promising, but caveats remain. Why might the seller be willing to take back a second mortgage? The answer could be any of a number of reasons. Maybe he or she sees you, the buyer, as a bird in the hand and just wants to do the deal and move on. Maybe the seller doesn't need all the proceeds at once and likes the idea of some ongoing cash flow from your mortgage payments.

Since I have been the prophet of doom for at least the last several pages, let me caution you about two other possibilities that you should keep in mind (after all, I didn't title this section, "Problem 4" for nothing). The first possibility is that it has been so difficult to find a buyer for this property that the seller feels compelled to offer some type of incentive in order to unload it. It might be wonderful to be on the receiving end of this incentive, but you shouldn't forget that as soon as you take title it will be you who now owns a property that is hard to sell.

Another reason that the seller could be happy to take back a second mortgage is because you're overpaying for the property. Part, maybe even all of the second loan amount, might be gravy from the seller's point of view, so why not take in the form of a note? The real lesson here is that you absolutely must do your homework and run your financial projections. Take my earlier admonitions seriously. When you buy an income property, you are buying a future income stream. Examine your projections carefully so you will know what to expect from that income stream.

Having said all this, are there circumstances where buying a property with no cash might prove to be a good move? It might seem odd, but one of the situations in which you would buy with all cash is also a time you could consider buying with no cash: when you expect to turn the property over for a considerable profit in a relatively short period of time. As we discussed above, you might see the opportunity to bring substantially subpar rents up to market rates. You might also see an opportunity to make physical changes to the property that could substantially increase rental income. (Be forewarned: Physical improvements by themselves do not really increase the value of an income property as they might for a single-family home. It is to the extent that those improvements increase the property's income stream that you'll realize an increase in value.)

If the profit potential from either of these two situations is great enough, then your overriding concern might be, "Can I close the deal?" Perhaps you have resources—cash or other assets—but you can't or don't want to tie them up in this venture. Your choices might then come down to these: "I pay the high costs involved in getting 100-percent financing; there is enough upside potential that I will still make a profit even if I have to pay those high financing costs for a short time," or "I'll pass and forego the potential profit."

Whenever you contemplate a no-cash deal, heed the following Rule of Thumb:

Rule of Thumb: Never purchase a property with no cash because you have no cash to invest. In other words, if you don't have two nickels to rub together, don't conjure up a creative financing scheme that allows you to buy an income property with no money down. Why? Because you're setting yourself up for a financial disaster. It should be a simple leap of logic to recognize that, if you bought the property with no money down because you had no money to put down, then when it comes time to make good on the property's negative cash flow, you'll be unable to do so.

For the sake of argument, however, let's say that by some miracle you do manage to cover the property's operating expenses and service its multiple debts with the rental income. A possible reason why this might occur is because the property's expenses are uncommonly low in relation to its income—perhaps because maintenance is being deferred. Whether it's your income property, your car, or your life, if you don't keep things in good order and repair, they start to fall apart. If you buy the property with no cash because you have no cash, then when you're faced with crucial repairs, you won't have money to put Humpty Dumpty back together. Do the math: No heat, no hot water equals no rent collection.

Some Cash

If you don't buy a property with all cash and don't buy it with no cash, then surely your one remaining option is to buy it with some cash. The most common model for the purchase of real estate, whether it is your primary residence or an investment property, is to use some amount of your own money as a down payment and finance the balance with a mortgage loan. At the risk of lapsing into pop philosophy, if most things happen for a reason, then there must be a reason why this is the most common approach to the purchase of real estate.

Actually, there are probably several reasons. The first and most obvious is that real estate is probably the most expensive purchase that you will ever make and it's quite likely that you don't have enough cash on hand to complete that purchase without the aid of financing. All cash might not be an option. Perhaps you have the funds but also have children in college or your own retirement on the horizon. It would be entirely rational for you to feel uncomfortable using that cash for investment purposes.

Using some cash and some financing is leverage in its classic form. Leverage, as it pertains to real estate, works like this:

You have at your disposal a given number of dollars to invest. You also have on your radar certain properties that you can buy. You could use all of your funds to buy one property, or you could take just some of that cash and combine it with financing to buy one property; then take another portion of the cash, combine it with additional financing to buy another property, and so on. Consider this example:

You have $100,000 to work with. Assume that if you finance a property you will need a 20-percent down payment. You plan to hold any properties you buy for three years, and you are confident that your prudent management along with general economic forces will allow you to resell each property for 10 percent more than you paid for it. In most real estate markets, such a projection would be conservative.

The key assumptions about leverage are these: The greatest economic benefit you are likely to achieve from your property will come from its increase in value, the gain you realize when you sell; and second, that gain is not dependent on the amount of cash you invest to purchase the property.

Case #1: You use all $100,000 to purchase a single property. When you resell, receive 10 percent more or $110,000.

Case #2: You use $20,000 as a down payment along with an $80,000 mortgage loan to purchase one property for $100,000. You repeat this process four more times, using up all of your $100,000 cash. Later you sell each of the five properties for $110,000 for a total gain of $50,000.

You used leverage to buy more property and create greater wealth. You amplified the strength of your cash by combining it with mortgage financing to buy five times as much property. *In each case, the value of the entire property went up, not just the value of your cash investment.*

This explanation is basically correct, but it is fraught with oversimplifications of which you should be wary. If you take this example at face value, you'll easily conclude that your best bet is to buy as many properties as possible with little or no cash down.

Mathematically this makes sense, but in real life there are issues. Leverage can be a very good thing, but as you saw in the previous section, there are reasons to be wary of leverage in its most extreme form, the no-cash deal. As financing approaches 100 percent of a property's value, that financing becomes increasingly expensive. The cost of financing is intimately connected to the risk involved. If you put 20 percent down on a property and finance 80 percent, you have a meaningful stake in that property and you will be very reluctant to walk away and abandon your 20 percent. But if you put nothing down and finance 100 percent, will you stand by this property (and pay your mortgage debt) in sickness and in health, in negative cash flow years as well as in good times? From the lender's point of view, the loan is much riskier if you the borrower don't have a significant financial commitment to the property. The lender, quite reasonably, expects to be compensated commensurately for that higher risk, and that extra compensation comes directly out of your pocket.

Another way of looking at the peril of this oversimplification is to see that it ignores your year-to-year cash flow and focuses, perhaps too intently, on the ultimate resale as your savior. Leverage is fundamentally a very good tool for a real estate investor, but when pushed to an extreme it can cause such damage to the year-by-year cash flow that it ends up cannibalizing its benefits.

> **Rule of Thumb:** *Never consider just the ultimate resale or just the ongoing cash flow when evaluating an income property investment. Project the entire income stream from the time you purchase until the time you might reasonably expect to sell. Look at the comparative case study below for guidance on how to do this.*

I discussed some special circumstances when an all-cash or no-cash deal might be desirable or even preferable, but if those circumstances don't apply then you will almost certainly be better off acquiring your real estate investment with conventional financing. This means you will typically put somewhere between 20 percent and 35 percent cash down and finance the rest with a first mortgage. A cash investment of this size represents sufficient security to the lender and lets you shop for the best terms among a wide range of competitors.

A Comparative Case Study

Did you ever have to make up your mind? Perhaps you've selected an investment property that you would like to purchase and find yourself in the enviable position of being able to choose among an all-cash, no-cash, or some-cash purchase. To help with such a decision, you'll find it very useful to create a series of pro-forma analyses (projections of future income, expenses, resale, etc.) where you test different scenarios related to the purchase of a given property to determine which will suit you best. By modeling your projections in this way, you can take some of the seat-of-the-pants out of your decision to use all cash, no cash, or some borrowed money.

Let's examine just such a set of alternatives. I'll use RealData's real estate investment software to run projections where you purchase a particular property at a discount for all cash, at no discount using no cash, and at no discount using conventional financing. For the sake of readability I'll extract small sections of the reports to display below. Here's the deal:

The property you have selected is a small apartment building with Gross Scheduled Rent of $57,600 in the first year. You assume you can increase the rents an average of 2.5 percent per year, but you also build in an allowance of 2 percent of the gross to account for income lost because of vacancy or due to rent that is uncollectible. You will incur operating expenses such as property taxes, insurance, maintenance, sewer, water, etc., that you estimate at $22,000 for the first year. You expect these costs to rise at 3 percent per year with the exception of the property taxes of $7500, which will rise 6 percent annually.

If you finance the property, you know you can purchase it for $300,000. However, you feel confident that if you offer the seller all cash, you can get the price down to $290,000. In either case, you will have to pay closing costs of $3000 when you take title on January 1, 2007.

If you choose to, you can obtain a first mortgage loan for 80 percent of the purchase price. It will have a term of 240 months with a variable interest rate that starts at 8 percent. You project that the rate will rise 1 percent each year from 2008 through 2011. You must pay 1 "point" (1 percent of the amount of the loan) as a premium up front to obtain the loan at that rate.

If you elect to use none of your own cash, then you will have to find a secondary lender that will give you enough money for the balance of the down payment, the closing costs, and the points. You can find such a loan, but of course it will be more expensive than the first mortgage. You identify a lender who will give you the loan for a term of 120 months, with an interest rate that starts at 11 percent, then goes up 1 percent each year thereafter. You must pay the lender four points to obtain this loan, but those points will be rolled into the loan amount.

Let's assume that you intend to hold the property for five years and then resell it. When you do so, you expect that its resale value will be based on its income stream at the time. Specifically, you project that the value will equal the property's Net Operating Income in the year of sale capitalized at 12 percent (i.e., NOI divided by 0.12). Investors in this market have actually been using an 11.5-percent rate to value apartment properties in this location, but you want to be prudent and conservative, so you predict that it's safer to assume that five years from now they might want a return that's a bit higher—hence your choice of 12 percent.

You will also have to pay a broker to find a buyer and a lawyer to close the transaction, and you assume that you'll pay 7 percent of the selling price for those services.

It's easy to see why you would rather use a computer than a yellow pad and calculator to build comparative pro formas. You know the particulars of three different scenarios: all cash, no cash, and some cash. Which scenario represents the best investment for you?

Let's look at the numbers over your 5-year holding period. You start with $57,600 in Gross Income, decrease it by 2 percent for Vacancy and Credit loss, then decrease it further by your first-year operating expenses of $22,000. Each year your Gross Income rises by 2.5 percent; most of your operating expenses rise by 3 percent, except for taxes, which increase by 6 percent. Your projected Annual Property Operating Data (APOD) for the next five years should look something like this (see Table 7.1).

No matter what the price of the property or the financing, your Net Operating Income will equal the Gross Operating Income less the Operating Expenses (see Table 7.2).

Before you go any further, take a look at the Net Operating Income. Recall you observed that investors were currently valuing this type of property by applying an 11.5 percent capitalization rate to the Net Operating Income.

Value = Net Operating Income / Capitalization Rate

Does the $290,000 to $300,000 price range that you expect to pay seem realistic? Plug in the first-year NOI and the 11.5 percent capitalization rate:

Value = 34,448 / 0.115 = $299,548

Valuation is not a precise science. This calculation suggests that the $290,000 to $300,000 price range is indeed realistic.

Now let's consider the three different purchase scenarios in detail. What

TABLE 7.1   Sample Property, Annual Property Operating Data

	2007	2008	2009	2010	2011
INCOME					
Gross Scheduled Rent Income	57,600	59,040	60,516	62,028	63,579
TOTAL GROSS INCOME	57,600	59,040	60,516	62,028	63,579
VACANCY & CREDIT ALLOWANCE	1,152	1,181	1,210	1,241	1,272
GROSS OPERATING INCOME	56,448	57,859	59,306	60,787	62,307
EXPENSES					
Accounting	600	618	637	656	676
Insurance (fire and liab.)	2,500	2,575	2,652	2,732	2,814
Lawn/Snow	200	206	212	218	225
Repairs and Maintenance	5,000	5,150	5,305	5,464	5,628
Supplies	1,000	1,030	1,061	1,093	1,126
Taxes					
Real Estate	7,500	7,950	8,427	8,933	9,469
Trash Removal	1,800	1,854	1,910	1,967	2,026
Utilities					
Electricity	1,200	1,236	1,273	1,311	1,350
Sewer and Water	2,200	2,266	2,334	2,404	2,476
TOTAL EXPENSES	22,000	22,885	23,811	24,778	25,790
NET OPERATING INCOME	34,448	34,974	35,495	36,009	36,517

TABLE 7.2   Sample Property, Net Operating Income (NOI)

	2007	2008	2009	2010	2011
GROSS INCOME	57,600	59,040	60,516	62,028	63,579
- Vacancy & Credit Allowance	1,152	1,181	1,210	1,241	1,272
- Operating Expenses	22,000	22,885	23,811	24,778	25,790
NET OPERATING INCOME	34,448	34,974	35,495	36,009	36,517

does your cash flow look like if you purchase this property for all cash? No
surprises here. You need a total of $293,000 to close the deal—$290,000 for
the purchase price and $3000 for the closing costs. You have no mortgage
payments, so your cash flow is the same as your NOI (see Table 7.3).

Notice also that your cash-on-cash return (i.e., your cash flow as a percentage of your initial cash investment), hovers around a respectable 12 percent.

What happens to your cash flow if you use none of your own cash and
finance everything? Remember, now you have both a first and a second
mortgage, including the points you must pay on each. In addition, you don't

TABLE 7.3 All Cash

	2007	2008	2009	2010	2011
NET OPERATING INCOME	34,448	34,974	35,495	36,009	36,517
- Debt Service, 1st Mortgage	0	0	0	0	0
- Debt Service, 2d Mortgage	0	0	0	0	0
- Debt Service, 3d Mortgage	0	0	0	0	0
- Debt Service, Refinance	0	0	0	0	0
CASH FLOW BEFORE TAXES	34,448	34,974	35,495	36,009	36,517
Cash on Cash Return (CFBT/Initial inv)	11.76%	11.94%	12.11%	12.29%	12.46%
Cumulative Cash Flow before Taxes	34,448	69,422	104,917	140,926	177,443

TABLE 7.4 No Cash

	2007	2008	2009	2010	2011
NET OPERATING INCOME	34,448	34,974	35,495	36,009	36,517
- Debt Service, 1st Mortgage	24,090	25,849	27,599	29,333	31,045
- Debt Service, 2d Mortgage	11,261	11,691	12,090	12,454	12,780
- Debt Service, 3d Mortgage	0	0	0	0	0
- Debt Service, Refinance	0	0	0	0	0
CASH FLOW BEFORE TAXES	(903)	(2,566)	(4,194)	(5,778)	(7,308)
Cash on Cash Return (CFBT/Initial inv)					
Cumulative Cash Flow before Taxes	(903)	(3,469)	(7,663)	(13,441)	(20,749)

have the bargaining leverage of an all-cash purchase and will pay $300,000 for the property (see Table 7.4).

This is ugly; and the funny thing about this no-cash deal is that you're looking at almost $21,000 in negative cash flows over five years. That's $21,000 you'll have to take out of your own pocket. Can you afford to do that? Pay me now or pay me later.

Notice also that you don't see a calculation of the cash-on-cash return. Why not? Because you can't calculate the return on nothing. "Cash-on-cash" means cash flow divided by cash invested. As you probably recall from your algebra class of many years ago, any number divided by zero equals infinity. (Note: In the real software, you would see an error here.)

Now let's look at the middle road. You use some cash and finance the rest. If you finance 80 percent of the $300,000 purchase price, you'll have to come up with a down payment of $60,000 as well as $3000 in closing costs and $2400 in points. When you do that, you'll still have the first mortgage payment shown in the previous scenario, but you won't have a second mortgage loan or the accompanying points to pay, so your cash flow will look like see Table 7.5.

TABLE 7.5   Some Cash

	2007	2008	2009	2010	2011
NET OPERATING INCOME	34,448	34,974	35,495	36,009	36,517
- Debt Service, 1st Mortgage	24,090	25,849	27,599	29,333	31,045
- Debt Service, 2d Mortgage	0	0	0	0	0
- Debt Service, 3d Mortgage	0	0	0	0	0
- Debt Service, Refinance	0	0	0	0	0
CASH FLOW BEFORE TAXES	10,358	9,125	7,896	6,676	5,472
Cash on Cash Return (CFBT/Initial inv)	15.84%	13.95%	12.07%	10.21%	8.37%
Cumulative Cash Flow before Taxes	10,358	19,483	27,379	34,055	39,527

These numbers are positive. That means you can take money out each year. In the short term, at least, that's likely to make you a lot happier than the so-called no-cash deal, which would have required you to support the property each year from your personal funds. You see that the cash flow declines each year. That's because your predicted rising interest rate is causing your debt service to increase. Even so, over the five-year period you experience a total *positive* cash flow of almost $40,000.

Cash flow is a good thing, but it's not the only thing. Those of you who have been faithful students of *What Every Real Estate Investor Needs to Know About Cash Flow* will recognize that there are other elements in these three investment pro formas that merit attention. For example, you haven't looked at the resale of the property yet, and you've given no consideration to the fact that there is a time value to money.

Let's look at the resale first. You plan to sell this property in five years. When you do, you can expect to pay an attorney to handle the closing and possibly a broker to find a buyer. You call these items "Costs of Sale." These costs, along with the balances outstanding on your mortgage loans, diminish the cash from sale to give you the "Before-Tax Sale Proceeds." You can think of the proceeds of sale as the very last cash flow you'll receive from this property because that's exactly what it is. Take a look at the output from the investment analysis software again to see what kind of proceeds you'll receive from each of your three scenarios.

First, all cash (see Table 7.6).

Recall that, at the beginning of this case study, I said you would project the eventual selling price of the property by applying a 12-percent capitalization rate to the Net Operating Income in the year of sale. As you've seen in several of the report snippets above, the NOI in year 5 (2011) is $36,517.

TABLE 7.6   All Cash

	2007	2008	2009	2010	2011
PROJECTED SELLING PRICE	287,000	291,000	296,000	300,000	304,000
- Costs of Sale	20,090	20,370	20,720	21,000	21,280
- 1st Mortgage Payoff	0	0	0	0	0
- 2d Mortgage Payoff	0	0	0	0	0
BEFORE-TAX SALE PROCEEDS	266,910	270,630	275,280	279,000	282,720

To review, the value formula is

Value = Net Operating Income / Capitalization Rate

So,

Value = 36,517 / 0.12 = 304,308, or $304,000 rounded to the nearest
thousand

From this amount you subtract the costs of sale, which you estimate as 7 percent of the selling price, to derive your final cash flow, the sale proceeds of $282,720.

Keep in mind that, because you had no debt, you've enjoyed substantial cash flows while operating the property each year—$177,443 in fact. You anted up $293,000 on day one to pay for the property and the closing costs. Ignoring for now the time value of money, you have, over five years taken out $177,443 in annual cash flows plus $282,720 in sale proceeds for a total of $460,163. Subtract your $293,000 initial investment and you're ahead of the game by $167,163.

Now, you can try the same calculations in regard to the no-cash and partial-cash deals. Here are a few clues: At the end of the fifth year, the balance of the first mortgage loan is $215,559. If you used no cash and borrowed the rest as a second mortgage, the balance of that loan is $44,766. I'll wait patiently while you scribble figures in the margin. Then I'll come back and discuss the results.

Hmmmm.....

OK. The selling price is going to remain the same in all of your scenarios and so are the costs of sale. As in the previous example, you'll have $282,720 in hand before you pay off any mortgages. Of course, in the all-cash deal you had no mortgages to pay off, so that amount represents your sale proceeds. If you purchase with no cash you'll now have two mortgages to pay off (see Table 7.7).

TABLE 7.7   No Cash

	2007	2008	2009	2010	2011
PROJECTED SELLING PRICE	287,000	291,000	296,000	300,000	304,000
- Costs of Sale	20,090	20,370	20,720	21,000	21,280
- 1st Mortgage Payoff	234,928	230,024	225,211	220,415	215,559
- 2d Mortgage Payoff	64,162	59,943	55,380	50,366	44,766
BEFORE-TAX SALE PROCEEDS	(32,180)	(19,337)	(5,311)	8,219	22,395

You're left with $22,395 from the sale. Recall that you have had to support the property to the tune of $20,749 for the past five years. You're ahead by a scant $1646.

If you purchased with some cash (i.e., just a first mortgage), you'll have to pay that off (see Table 7.8).

TABLE 7.8   Some Cash

	2007	2008	2009	2010	2011
PROJECTED SELLING PRICE	287,000	291,000	296,000	300,000	304,000
- Costs of Sale	20,090	20,370	20,720	21,000	21,280
- 1st Mortgage Payoff	234,928	230,024	225,211	220,415	215,559
BEFORE-TAX SALE PROCEEDS	31,982	40,606	50,069	58,585	67,161

You go home with a check for $67,161. During the five years you've owned the property, you enjoyed $39,527 in positive cash flows (see the cash flow worksheet above), so you've taken at total of $106,688 out of the property. Your initial investment included the down payment of $60,000, closing costs of $3000, and loan points of $2400—a total of $65,400, leaving you ahead by $41,288.

Let's organize the information you've collected so far into a format that is more readable for the purpose of comparison. Recall I suggested earlier that you should think of the Proceeds of Sale as just another cash flow. That's true, and you can also think of your initial cash investment as a cash flow. A very simple and readable way of organizing the kind of data we've produced is to lay it out in the form of yearly cash flows.

A standard technique among real estate investors when making pro forma projections is to annualize a property's cash flows; that is, to treat them as if they occur in a lump sum at the end of each year. It's probably true that you don't really collect all your rents and pay all your bills on New Year's Eve, and beginning investors sometimes question whether annualizing is a sound approach. You must keep in mind that a pro forma is an estimate of what will happen in the future, not a precise accounting of what has occurred in the past. If, in an effort to improve accuracy, you try to make such estimates on a monthly basis, then you would have to make 12 times as many projections of future income and expense. That would add significantly to the time needed to complete a pro forma. Rather than improving the quality of projections, that additional effort might actually cause it to decline because you have far greater "degrees of freedom" in your projections. In other words, the probable errors you would introduce by having to make many more predictions would likely offset the benefit of fine-tuning the timing.

If you're still not convinced, consider that the most likely recipient of any pro forma you might produce (lender, partner, broker) would probably be surprised to see it in anything but an annualized format and find it difficult to absorb. Cliché notwithstanding, sometimes less really is more.

Now that you have been browbeaten into agreement, I'll point out one exception to the end-of-year (EOY) lump sum amount and that is the beginning of year (BOY) amount. The most common use of this in real estate is to express your initial investment as a negative cash flow that occurs BOY1—beginning of year 1.

Now look at these properties as a simple comparison of cash flows (see Table 7.9).

TABLE 7.9   Cash Flow Comparison

	All Cash	No Cash	Some Cash
BOY1	(293,000)	0	(65,400)
EOY1	34,448	(903)	10,358
EOY2	34,974	(2,566)	9,125
EOY3	35,495	(4,194)	7,896
EOY4	36,009	(5,778)	6,676
EOY5	319,237	15,087	72,633
Total $	$167,163	$1,646	$41,288

Notice that the EOY5 cash flows appear to display numbers you haven't seen before. Remember that you are selling the property in the fifth year, so for that year you really have two cash flows combined—one from the regular operation of the property and one from the proceeds of the sale. For example, the "all-cash" property has a fifth-year operating cash flow of $36,517, which combines with the sale proceeds of $282,720 to comprise the EOY5 cash flow shown.

What useful information can you get from this chart? Can this help you to choose your method of purchase? One item that stands out is how weak the no-cash scenario looks when compared to the others. True, it cost you nothing to get into this deal—nothing at BOY1, that is. But you immediately began using your own money to offset negative cash flows. Notice also that the cash flows get worse each year as your financing costs rise. Only the eventual resale bails you out, and then just barely. What if you have a few unexpected leaky water heaters over five years of ownership? You could spend five years working at being a landlord and end up with nothing to show for it.

The other number that jumps out is your total positive cash flow from the all-cash deal. It would certainly appear that you're much farther ahead with the all-cash deal. Is that the best choice?

So far you have been looking at dollars in absolute terms, with no regard to when you paid them or when you received them. Would you be happy if I told you that you had just won $1 million in the lottery? Would you still be happy if I explained that the payout would be $1 per year for a million years?

There is a time value to money, and it has a significant impact on your investment decisions. Money received in the future is less valuable than the same amount received today. Conversely, money paid out in the future is lest costly than money paid out today.

There are techniques you can use that will help you look at the property's entire income stream from day of purchase to day of sale and take into account both the magnitude and the timing of the various cash flows that occur along the way. The metric of choice among most investors is Internal Rate of Return, so it's worthwhile to digress for a moment on this subject. IRR will take heed of not only the amount of the year-to-year cash flows but also when they occur; and it will incorporate the amount of the initial investment and recognize how long you must wait to receive the eventual proceeds of sale. IRR is particularly well suited to situations where you are comparing alternative investments or comparing different scenarios for a single property precisely because it does pay attention to the timing and amount of all cash in and all cash out.

IRR is the single rate at which you can discount all future returns back to day one so that their total equals the amount of the initial investment.

Picture the concept this way: You invest a certain amount of cash on day one. What you buy with that money is a series of cash flows that occur in different amounts and at different times in the future. What is the one, unique interest rate that would allow you to receive exactly those returns at exactly those times? That rate is the Internal Rate of Return.

It's not something you'll scratch out on the back of an envelope. You'll need a financial calculator or computer software. You can download a simple Excel model at realdata.com/secrets for this purpose. When you enter an initial investment and a series of cash flows, the model uses Excel's built-in IRR function to compute the overall rate of return.

IRR is sensitive to the fact that money received in the future is not as valuable as money received in the present. If you have to wait a long time to achieve what appears to be success with an investment, you may in fact not be doing as well as if you earned fewer dollars but received them sooner. You can use the IRR Excel model to see this point. Consider the following. The property produces a modest but positive cash flow every year, and then in year 10, when you sell, it yields a seemingly handsome profit. A good investment? The IRR is only 5.82 percent, probably quite low compared to your investment goals. The reason it's so low is that you will have to wait 10 years before you receive the cash flow from resale. The gain in value might look large, but it occurs so far into the future that it value today—its *present value*, as it's called—is far less. See Table 7.10.

TABLE 7.10   Internal Rate of Return, Sale EOY 10

Initial Investment	100,000
Cash Flow, End of Year 1	2,000
Cash Flow, End of Year 2	1,500
Cash Flow, End of Year 3	1,750
Cash Flow, End of Year 4	2,000
Cash Flow, End of Year 5	2,250
Cash Flow, End of Year 6	3,300
Cash Flow, End of Year 7	3,750
Cash Flow, End of Year 8	4,500
Cash Flow, End of Year 9	6,000
Cash Flow, End of Year 10	142,000

Internal Rate of Return	5.82%

TABLE 7.11   Internal Rate of Return, Sale EOY 3

Initial Investment	100,000
Cash Flow, End of Year 1	2,000
Cash Flow, End of Year 2	1,500
Cash Flow, End of Year 3	142,000
Cash Flow, End of Year 4	0
Cash Flow, End of Year 5	0
Cash Flow, End of Year 6	0
Cash Flow, End of Year 7	0
Cash Flow, End of Year 8	0
Cash Flow, End of Year 9	0
Cash Flow, End of Year 10	0
Internal Rate of Return	13.52%

You can experiment with this template to get a feel for how timing and amount interact to make up your rate of return. Try moving the $142,000 sale-year cash flow up to Year 3 instead of Year 10 (Table 7.11).

Your return is substantially greater because you'll receive the largest cash flow in a shorter time.

What can IRR tell you about your three alternatives for purchasing this property? Earlier you saw how to calculate the cash flows from operating the property each year and the cash proceeds from selling the property. If you take a larger slice from the software reports excerpted above, you can see the IRR you would achieve by buying with all, no, or some cash and holding the property from one to five years (Table 7.12).

If you're figuring your cash flows and sale proceeds manually, you can still use the IRR template to calculate your rate of return. Recall that we summarized the cash flows from each scenario as shown in Table 7.13.

Take the all-cash numbers and plug them into the IRR template to see what happens if you sell at the end of Year 5 (Table 7.14).

The IRR analysis of these three ways of structuring this deal is enlightening. The no-cash proposition for this particular property is clearly the weakest. You'll have negative cash flow from operating the property and actually lose money if you sell during the first four years. The all-cash deal takes a year to ramp up, but after that the rate of return is solid. You could safely sell at any time after the first year. The conventionally financed pur-

TABLE 7.12 Sample Property IRR; All, No, Some Cash

	2007	2008	2009	2010	2011
PROJECTED SELLING PRICE	287,000	291,000	296,000	300,000	304,000
- Costs of Sale	20,090	20,370	20,720	21,000	21,280
- 1st Mortgage Payoff	0	0	0	0	0
- 2d Mortgage Payoff	0	0	0	0	0
BEFORE-TAX SALE PROCEEDS	266,910	270,630	275,280	279,000	282,720
Internal Rate of Return (Before Tax)	2.85%	8.18%	10.10%	10.99%	11.52%

All Cash

	2007	2008	2009	2010	2011
PROJECTED SELLING PRICE	287,000	291,000	296,000	300,000	304,000
- Costs of Sale	20,090	20,370	20,720	21,000	21,280
- 1st Mortgage Payoff	234,928	230,024	225,211	220,415	215,559
- 2d Mortgage Payoff	64,162	59,943	55,380	50,366	44,766
BEFORE-TAX SALE PROCEEDS	(32,180)	(19,337)	(5,311)	8,219	22,395
Internal Rate of Return (Before Tax)	n/a	n/a	n/a	n/a	6.19%

No Cash

	2007	2008	2009	2010	2011
PROJECTED SELLING PRICE	287,000	291,000	296,000	300,000	304,000
- Costs of Sale	20,090	20,370	20,720	21,000	21,280
- 1st Mortgage Payoff	234,928	230,024	225,211	220,415	215,559
BEFORE-TAX SALE PROCEEDS	31,982	40,606	50,069	58,585	67,161
Internal Rate of Return (Before Tax)	-35.26%	-4.52%	6.72%	11.05%	12.96%

Some Cash

chase starts off slow but gains ground quickly. By the end of the fifth year, it shows the strongest rate of return.

> ***Rule of Thumb:*** *Does all this prove that using some cash and some financing is always the best approach and using no cash always the worst? If you were to run the kind of analyses you've done here on a hundred deals, you would probably find that the "some cash, some financing" model would prevail over the others more often than not. On a given day, however, you'll be buying a building, not a generalization. The more important lesson here is that you must*

TABLE 7.13   Cash Flow Comparison

	All Cash	No Cash	Some Cash
BOY1	(293,000)	0	(65,400)
EOY1	34,448	(903)	10,358
EOY2	34,974	(2,566)	9,125
EOY3	35,495	(4,194)	7,896
EOY4	36,009	(5,778)	6,676
EOY5	319,237	15,087	72,633
Total $	$167,163	$1,646	$41,288

TABLE 7.14   IRR, All Cash Scenario

Initial Investment	293,000
Cash Flow, End of Year 1	34,448
Cash Flow, End of Year 2	34,974
Cash Flow, End of Year 3	35,495
Cash Flow, End of Year 4	36,009
Cash Flow, End of Year 5	319,237
Cash Flow, End of Year 6	0
Cash Flow, End of Year 7	0
Cash Flow, End of Year 8	0
Cash Flow, End of Year 9	0
Cash Flow, End of Year 10	0

Internal Rate of Return   11.52%

look at the property as an income stream and analyze that income
stream to see if you can reasonably expect it to provide an acceptable return on your investment. You can compare different properties or, as we've done here, you can compare different methods of
structuring the transaction for a single property. You can try best-
case / worst-case / most-likely variations as well to see how different purchase prices, financing, or resale assumptions might impact
your results. The more you work with developing projections, the
more proficient you'll become at making and evaluating them. The
harder you work at this, the luckier you'll become.

8

Line Them Up Again—Comparing Loans

When you were choosing a property, you lined them up for the sake of direct comparison. Selecting the right loan is a close second in importance, so it's no less essential for you to make a side-by-side assessment of what each lender has to offer. Make copies of Table 8.1 and use them to collect information about each of your potential sources of financing.

Keep in mind that loan terms, especially interest rates, can change on a daily basis. You can find terms published in newspapers and periodicals or on Web sites like bankrate.com. If you want to use those resources, then use them to develop your short list of potential lenders, but don't rely on the quoted terms as being current. One exception: Some lenders will stamp the exact date and time of the last rate update on their Web sites so you can determine just how up-to-date the information is.

> *Rule of Thumb: As a rule, however, you'll want to pick up the telephone and get this information directly from a mortgage lender or broker. Be certain that you have your checklist in hand when you call. Not only will it ensure that you don't overlook any key items,*

TABLE 8.1   Potential Sources of Financing

	Lender:	Lender:	Lender:	Lender:
Loan-to-Value Ratio				
Maximum Loan $				
Down Pmt. Required				
Debt Coverage Ratio				
Initial Interest Rate				
Fixed?				
ARM?				
Adjustment Interval				
Index				
Margin				
Maximum Adjustment				
Rate Cap				
Initial Payment				
Maximum Term				
Balloon				
Points				
Points, $				
Lock-Out Period				
Pre-Payment Penalty				
Assumable?				
Recourse?				
Funded Reserves?				
Total Lender Fees				
3d-Party Fees				
Appraisal				
Credit Report				
Courier				
Flood Certification				
Survey				
Other				
Legal & Closing Fees				
Attorney/Settlement				
Title Insurance				
Recording				
Tax Stamps				

*but it will also establish you as a person who knows what questions
to ask. Even if you are a beginner, that's no reason to act like one.*

You saw most of the items on Table 8.1 discussed in earlier chapters, so
just a few remarks are needed here. The Loan-to-Value and Debt Coverage
ratios are among the most important items you need to know, so they are
near the top of the list. The line called, "Maximum Loan Amount" is provided so you can translate that percentage into dollars for your own benefit. As you do so, you might also want to ask something like, "I assume, if
everything else is in order, that $800,000 on a strip center is within your
lending guidelines." Occasionally a small local lender might lack the capac-
ity to underwrite a large loan. Better to ask than to waste time.

The "Down Payment Required" is not a question you need to ask the
lender. It's obviously the difference between the maximum loan amount and
the purchase price of the property. I've provided this line on the form to help
you keep focused on the number of dollars you need to go into this deal.

The "Adjustment Interval" refers to an Adjustable Rate Mortgage. How
often can the rate change? Every 6 months? Every 12? Some loans have
floating rates and adjust whenever the index to which they are tied goes up
or down. Earlier I discussed something called a "Fixed to Arm" in which
the rate is fixed for a certain number of years and then becomes adjustable.
An easy way to express a loan like this on your chart is in a form such as
"3/1," signifying that the first adjustment occurs at the end of 3 years and
is followed by an adjustment every 1 year thereafter.

You also want to know how much the rate can change. That is usually
expressed as a maximum increase per adjustment and a maximum rate or
"cap" over the life of the loan. It's possible, of course, that the particular
loan might have no limits.

In regard to Lender Fees, I've provided just one line. As discussed
above, you won't accomplish much by wrestling over the inclusion, exclu-
sion, or amount of any of the various fees that lenders and brokers charge
for originating, underwriting, processing, documenting, hallucinating, or
whatever else goes on before you get the check. Get the total of fees,
excluding those third-party and legal costs, accounted for elsewhere on the
form.

Some lenders might require that you have a "funded reserves" account.
This is an account you establish and fund on day one. It might be earmarked

to provide a cushion against future cash flow emergencies (caused, for example, by an unanticipated vacancy) or for future capital expenditures (such as a new roof). This is not really a loan cost because it remains your money. Nonetheless, it can represent additional cash you need in order to close the deal.

In choosing the right loan, one size does not fit all. Your first criterion must be to find a lender that will give you enough money to close the deal. Great terms won't help if the loan is too small, so LTV and DCR are of paramount importance. After that you'll be dealing with trade-offs. Do you want the lowest rate with frequent adjustments or a higher rate locked in for a longer time? Are you comfortable with a balloon loan if it means paying no points or lower fees?

> ***Rule of Thumb:*** *Questions like those above don't have universal right answers, but very often your best choices will revolve around how long you plan to hold the property and the mortgage. If you expect to sell in a relatively short time (say, less than 5 years) and have an opportunity to reduce your up-front loan costs by agreeing to a balloon payment, your choice is clear. You'll probably sell before the balloon comes due, and you definitely don't want to load up a short period of ownership with high initial fees. On the other hand, if you don't believe you'll sell in the near future, you might prefer to pay a higher rate in order to guarantee that the rate stays fixed for an extended time.*

9

How Do You Convince a Lender to Finance Your Real Estate Investment?

Unless you are in the position of having both adequate funds and sufficient reason to buy an investment property for all cash, you'll be looking for a mortgage loan to complete the deal. As you saw earlier, the first part of the process is to identify the best loan for your circumstances—the right mix of rate, term, fees, and conditions. Once you've found what you're looking for, the second task (in real estate as in life) is to get it.

Can You Qualify?

When you purchase a home, the lender is interested in your creditworthiness and in whether or not you have enough income to make the payments. As discussed earlier, when you buy an investment property, the lender usually cares if the property has enough income to cover the payments but still wants to know that you, the borrower, are a good risk. "Deadbeat" is not something you would put on your resume. If you have a history of not paying your bills on time or at all, if you live month-to-month making minimum payments on a stack of credit cards, don't be surprised to find that someone has rolled up the welcome mat and put it away.

A good place to start your investment program—before you shop for properties and before you apply for a loan—is to investigate your credit before anyone else does. You can start by pulling your own credit reports' and checking out your FICO score. FICO is a credit risk score that most lenders use. It was developed in the 1950s by the Fair Isaac Co., hence FICO. You can find out more about them at www.fairisaac.com.

There are three major reporting agencies (also referred to as credit bureaus), any or all of which your lender can use: Equifax, Experian, and TransUnion. The data in a credit report includes the following:

1. Identification—your name, address, social security number, date of birth
2. Credit history—past and current car loans, mortgages, credit cards, etc., along with current balances, credit limits, and payment histories
3. Inquiries—a record of all accesses of your credit report over the past two years
4. Public record information—bankruptcies, lawsuits, liens, judgments, etc.

The three agencies will also report a score, based on the Fair Isaac system. The scores might not be the same because the agencies don't necessarily each have exactly the same pool of information about your credit history. Individual lenders might use this score as-is or might integrate it into a scoring system of their own when they make underwriting decisions.

To purchase copies of your credit reports and obtain your FICO scores, you can go to their consumer site, www.myfico.com. These reports are also available from each of the individual bureaus (just add dot-com to each of the company names). You can and should examine all three reports and scores. When you're headed off to an important meeting, you probably stop before you leave home to check yourself in the mirror. Hair combed, moustache trimmed, lipstick straight? (Adjust for gender, as necessary.) You need to know how you look to the creditors of the world as well. Check not only to uncover errors in what the bureaus might be reporting about you, but also to know what these reports contain that might be accurate but unflattering. Look for information that is incorrect, and if you find something, file a dispute. In particular, be on the lookout for accounts and loans that you have paid off but that still show as open. Also, look for duplicate records.

An intriguing tool offered by MyFico is their Score Simulator™. This allows you to see an approximation of what would happen to your score if you improved your on-time payment of bills, missed a payment on an account that is current, declared bankruptcy, paid down your credit cards, maxed out your cards, applied for new credit, or transferred credit card balances.

Your FICO score can affect not only your ability to obtain a loan; it can also affect the rate you'll pay if you do get the loan. Yet another interesting tool you'll find at the MyFico site is their Loan Savings Calculator. For several ranges of FICO scores, you can see the average Annual Percentage Rate paid for mortgages as well as home-equity loans and auto loans. For example, as I write this I find that I might pay just under 6.25 percent for a $300,000 30-year fixed-rate mortgage in Connecticut if my FICO score is over 720 compared to more than 9.5 percent for a score in the low to mid 500s. Just in case I missed the point, they allow me to plug in my score range and show that I could save tens of thousands of dollars in interest over the term of the loan if my score were higher or pay tens or even hundreds of thousands more if my score were lower.

One final bit of late-breaking news: Congress passed The Fair and Accurate Credit Transactions Act in December, 2003. The Act gives every citizen the right to receive a copy of his or her credit report every year at no charge from each of the three bureaus. The Act also gave the FTC six months to figure out how this is going to be accomplished and the credit bureaus another six months to comply. If all goes according to plan, you should be able to obtain your free reports by the end of 2004. In the meantime, if you're in hot pursuit of an investment property mortgage, pay the small fee to obtain your report now.

How to Make a World-Class Loan Presentation

Mortgage officers and loan underwriters see a lot of proposals come across their desks. Gaining approval for an investment-property loan is not as arduous as, say, getting a book published (editor, please note), but it is nonetheless a process that demands careful preparation and a well-designed presentation. You can choose to walk into a lender cold or to arrive with a "loan package" in hand. When you come in prepared, you accomplish two objectives: You make the lender's job easier and hence the decision process quicker; perhaps more important, you establish your own credibility and thereby increase your overall chances of success.

Applying for an investment loan without preparation is the mark of an amateur. That's not how you want to be seen. If you're ready to approach a lender to finance a deal, that means you have already researched several sources of funding, as described in the earlier section, "Line Them Up Again—Comparing Loans." You know their underwriting requirements, such as Loan-to-Value and Debt Coverage Ratios. Now you need to put together an effective presentation package.

What should go into your recipe for a spell-casting presentation? Get out your boiling cauldron and start to stir:

> Eye of newt, and toe of frog,
> Wool of bat, and tongue of dog,
> Adder's fork, and blind-worm's sting,
> Lizard's leg, and howlet's wing,
> For a charm of powerful trouble,
> Like a hell-broth boil and bubble.
>
> Shakespeare's *Macbeth* (IV, i, 14–15)

Wrong checklist. That goes with the three witches, not the three credit bureaus. The real recipe, while it varies a bit from lender to lender, will include many of the less exotic ingredients listed below. The lender will require some of these items, but the smart borrower will arrive with many of the others in hand. See the Loan Package Checklist.

About the Borrower

The first item—personal background and experience—is part cover letter, part curriculum vitae. In this age of automated underwriting, it might seem quaint to humanize the application in this way. Don't dismiss the value of proclaiming your personal qualifications. If you have owned and/or man-

Loan Package Checklist

About the Borrower:

_____ Personal background, experience _____

_____ FNMA form 1003 _____

_____ Income Tax Returns (last two years; all schedules including K-1s)

    _____ Personal _____

    _____ Business _____

    _____ Partnerships _____

    _____ W-2s, last two years _____

_____ Recent pay stubs _____

_____ Personal Financial Statement _____

About the Property:

_____ Purchase contract _____

_____ Leases, estoppel certs. _____

_____ Property Pro Forma

    _____ Rent Roll _____

    _____ APOD _____

    _____ Cash flow projections _____

    _____ Resale projections _____

    _____ Financial ratios & rates of return

        _____ Loan-to-Value Ratio _____

        _____ Debt Coverage Ratio _____

        _____ Internal Rate of Return _____

        _____ Present Value Analysis (DCF) _____

        _____ Capitalization Rate _____

        _____ Gross Rent Multiplier _____

        _____ Cash-on-Cash Return _____

        _____ Income and Expenses per SF _____

        _____ Vacancy and Credit Loss Allowance _____

aged investment real estate before, you should mention that fact. Describe any experience in business or finance. Job stability, education, civic activities—these items might not seem relevant to you at first, but they can be relevant to a lender who is assessing the degree of risk in making a loan. Consider a comment like this in the underwriter's file: "This applicant has never owned investment property, but runs her own business and has set up a profit-sharing plan for her employees. She owns her home, where she has lived for 12 years and serves on the local Zoning Board of Appeals." A few simple facts establish her competence in business and finance, stability, roots in the community, and experience with property-related issues. Before the lender even looks at the financials, it knows this is a credible applicant. In a borderline situation, that credibility could be enough to tip the scale toward approval.

> **Rule of Thumb:** *If your bona fides are not as impressive as the example above, don't invent or exaggerate. If you don't feel your background looks sufficiently stirring to put on paper, then it's better to forego this cover letter than to stretch the truth.*
>
> *Also, don't use the cover letter to try to explain away the problematic parts of your application or credit history. "The dog ate my homework" didn't convince your fourth-grade teacher. She now works for the mortgage department.*

FNMA form 1003 (Figure 9.1) is the standard application for loans on 1–4-family properties, so if that's the kind of property you're financing, expect to complete this form. Lenders must use the form if they want to sell the loan at some point on the secondary market. Even lenders who don't plan to sell the loan will usually use it. If you approach the lender with the form already filled out, you'll save the go-home-come-back-later step.

If you're financing a small residential property, you will probably need to provide your W-2s for the last two years as well as recent pay stubs. If the loan is fairly large, if you're self-employed, or if the property is a commercial or a larger residential piece, then you will typically have to provide copies of your tax returns for the past two years as well. My recommendation is to make the copies and bring them with you when you meet with the lender. If they're not needed, you can bring them home.

If you own 25 percent or more of a business, you'll have to provide two years' tax returns for that as well. Some lenders will also ask for a current

Uniform Residential Loan Application

This application is designed to be completed by the applicant(s) with the Lender's assistance. Applicants should complete this form as 'Borrower' or 'Co-Borrower,' as applicable. Co-Borrower information must also be provided (and the appropriate box checked) when ☐ the income or assets of a person other than the 'Borrower' (including the Borrower's spouse) will be used as a basis for loan qualification or ☐ the income or assets of the Borrower's spouse will not be used as a basis for loan qualification, but his or her liabilities must be considered because the Borrower resides in a community property state, the security property is located in a community property state, or the Borrower is relying on other property located in a community property state as a basis for repayment of the loan.

I. TYPE OF MORTGAGE AND TERMS OF LOAN

Mortgage Applied for:	☐ VA ☐ FHA	☐ Conventional ☐ USDA/Rural Housing Service	☐ Other (explain):	Agency Case Number	Lender Case Number

Amount $	Interest Rate %	No. of Months	Amortization Type:	☐ Fixed Rate ☐ GPM	☐ Other (explain): ☐ ARM (type):

II. PROPERTY INFORMATION AND PURPOSE OF LOAN

Subject Property Address (street, city, state, & ZIP)	No. of Units

Legal Description of Subject Property (attach description if necessary)	Year Built

Purpose of Loan	☐ Purchase ☐ Construction ☐ Refinance ☐ Construction-Permanent	☐ Other (explain):	Property will be: ☐ Primary Residence ☐ Secondary Residence ☐ Investment

Complete this line if construction or construction-permanent loan.

Year Lot Acquired	Original Cost $	Amount Existing Liens $	(a) Present Value of Lot $	(b) Cost of Improvements $	Total (a + b) $

Complete this line if this is a refinance loan.

Year Acquired	Original Cost $	Amount Existing Liens $	Purpose of Refinance	Describe Improvements ☐ made ☐ to be made Cost: $

Title will be held in what Name(s)	Manner in which Title will be held	Estate will be held in: ☐ Fee Simple ☐ Leasehold (show expiration date)

Source of Down Payment, Settlement Charges and/or Subordinate Financing (explain)

III. BORROWER INFORMATION

Borrower	Co-Borrower
Borrower's Name (include Jr. or Sr. if applicable)	Co-Borrower's Name (include Jr. or Sr. if applicable)
Social Security Number / Home Phone (incl. area code) / DOB (mm/dd/yyyy) / Yrs. School	Social Security Number / Home Phone (incl. area code) / DOB (mm/dd/yyyy) / Yrs. School
☐ Married ☐ Unmarried (include single, divorced, widowed) ☐ Separated / Dependents (not listed by Co-Borrower) no. ages	☐ Married ☐ Unmarried (include single, divorced, widowed) ☐ Separated / Dependents (not listed by Borrower) no. ages
Present Address (street, city, state, ZIP) ☐ Own ☐ Rent No. Yrs.	Present Address (street, city, state, ZIP) ☐ Own ☐ Rent No. Yrs.
Mailing Address, if different from Present Address	Mailing Address, if different from Present Address

If residing at present address for less than two years, complete the following:

Former Address (street, city, state, ZIP) ☐ Own ☐ Rent No. Yrs.	Former Address (street, city, state, ZIP) ☐ Own ☐ Rent No. Yrs.

IV. EMPLOYMENT INFORMATION

Borrower	Co-Borrower
Name & Address of Employer ☐ Self Employed / Yrs. on this job / Yrs. employed in this line of work/profession	Name & Address of Employer ☐ Self Employed / Yrs. on this job / Yrs. employed in this line of work/profession
Position/Title/Type of Business / Business Phone (incl. area code)	Position/Title/Type of Business / Business Phone (incl. area code)

If employed in current position for less than two years or if currently employed in more than one position, complete the following:

Name & Address of Employer ☐ Self Employed / Dates (from – to) / Monthly Income $	Name & Address of Employer ☐ Self Employed / Dates (from – to) / Monthly Income $
Position/Title/Type of Business / Business Phone (incl. area code)	Position/Title/Type of Business / Business Phone (incl. area code)
Name & Address of Employer ☐ Self Employed / Dates (from – to) / Monthly Income $	Name & Address of Employer ☐ Self Employed / Dates (from – to) / Monthly Income $
Position/Title/Type of Business / Business Phone (incl. area code)	Position/Title/Type of Business / Business Phone (incl. area code)

FIGURE 9.1   Uniform Residential Loan Application.

V. MONTHLY INCOME AND COMBINED HOUSING EXPENSE INFORMATION

Gross Monthly Income	Borrower	Co-Borrower	Total	Combined Monthly Housing Expense	Present	Proposed
Base Empl. Income*	$	$	$	Rent	$	
Overtime				First Mortgage (P&I)		$
Bonuses				Other Financing (P&I)		
Commissions				Hazard Insurance		
Dividends/Interest				Real Estate Taxes		
Net Rental Income				Mortgage Insurance		
Other (before completing, see the notice in "describe other income" below)				Homeowner Assn. Dues		
				Other:		
Total	$	$	$	Total	$	$

* Self Employed Borrower(s) may be required to provide additional documentation such as tax returns and financial statements.

Describe Other Income *Notice:* Alimony, child support, or separate maintenance income need not be revealed if the Borrower (B) or Co-Borrower (C) does not choose to have it considered for repaying this loan.

B/C		Monthly Amount
		$

VI. ASSETS AND LIABILITIES

This Statement and any applicable supporting schedules may be completed jointly by both married and unmarried Co-Borrowers if their assets and liabilities are sufficiently joined so that the Statement can be meaningfully and fairly presented on a combined basis; otherwise, separate Statements and Schedules are required. If the Co-Borrower section was completed about a spouse, this Statement and supporting schedules must be completed about that spouse also.

Completed ☐ Jointly ☐ Not Jointly

ASSETS Description	Cash or Market Value	Liabilities and Pledged Assets. List the creditor's name, address and account number for all outstanding debts, including automobile loans, revolving charge accounts, real estate loans, alimony, child support, stock pledges, etc. Use continuation sheet, if necessary. Indicate by (*) those liabilities which will be satisfied upon sale of real estate owned or upon refinancing of the subject property.		
Cash deposit toward purchase held by:	$			
		LIABILITIES	Monthly Payment & Months Left to Pay	Unpaid Balance
List checking and savings accounts below		Name and address of Company	$ Payment/Months	$
Name and address of Bank, S&L, or Credit Union				
		Acct. no.		
Acct. no.	$	Name and address of Company	$ Payment/Months	$
Name and address of Bank, S&L, or Credit Union				
		Acct. no.		
Acct. no.	$	Name and address of Company	$ Payment/Months	$
Name and address of Bank, S&L, or Credit Union				
		Acct. no.		
Acct. no.	$	Name and address of Company	$ Payment/Months	$
Name and address of Bank, S&L, or Credit Union				
		Acct. no.		
Acct. no.	$	Name and address of Company	$ Payment/Months	$
Stocks & Bonds (Company name/number & description)	$			
		Acct. no.		
Life insurance net cash value	$	Name and address of Company	$ Payment/Months	$
Face amount: $				
Subtotal Liquid Assets	$			
Real estate owned (enter market value from schedule of real estate owned)	$	Acct. no.		
Vested interest in retirement fund	$	Name and address of Company	$ Payment/Months	$
Net worth of business(es) owned (attach financial statement)	$			
Automobiles owned (make and year)	$	Acct. no.		
		Alimony/Child Support/Separate Maintenance Payments Owed to:	$	
Other Assets (itemize)	$	Job-Related Expense (child care, union dues, etc.)	$	
		Total Monthly Payments	$	
Total Assets a.	$	Net Worth (a minus b) ▶ $	Total Liabilities b.	$

FIGURE 9.1   Uniform Residential Loan Application.

VI. ASSETS AND LIABILITIES (cont.)

Schedule of Real Estate Owned (If additional properties are owned, use continuation sheet.)

Property Address (enter S if sold, PS if pending sale or R if rental being held for income) ➡	Type of Property	Present Market Value	Amount of Mortgages & Liens	Gross Rental Income	Mortgage Payments	Insurance, Maintenance, Taxes & Misc.	Net Rental Income
		$	$	$	$	$	$
	Totals	$	$	$	$	$	$

List any additional names under which credit has previously been received and indicate appropriate creditor name(s) and account number(s):

Alternate Name	Creditor Name	Account Number

VII. DETAILS OF TRANSACTION

a. Purchase price	$
b. Alterations, improvements, repairs	
c. Land (if acquired separately)	
d. Refinance (incl. debts to be paid off)	
e. Estimated prepaid items	
f. Estimated closing costs	
g. PMI, MIP, Funding Fee	
h. Discount (if Borrower will pay)	
i. Total costs (add items a through h)	
j. Subordinate financing	
k. Borrower's closing costs paid by Seller	
l. Other Credits (explain)	
m. Loan amount (exclude PMI, MIP, Funding Fee financed)	
n. PMI, MIP, Funding Fee financed	
o. Loan amount (add m & n)	
p. Cash from/to Borrower (subtract j, k, l & o from i)	

VIII. DECLARATIONS

If you answer "Yes" to any questions a through i, please use continuation sheet for explanation.

	Borrower Yes	Borrower No	Co-Borrower Yes	Co-Borrower No
a. Are there any outstanding judgments against you?	☐	☐	☐	☐
b. Have you been declared bankrupt within the past 7 years?	☐	☐	☐	☐
c. Have you had property foreclosed upon or given title or deed in lieu thereof in the last 7 years?	☐	☐	☐	☐
d. Are you a party to a lawsuit?	☐	☐	☐	☐
e. Have you directly or indirectly been obligated on any loan which resulted in foreclosure, transfer of title in lieu of foreclosure, or judgment? (This would include such loans as home mortgage loans, SBA loans, home improvement loans, educational loans, manufactured (mobile) home loans, any mortgage, financial obligation, bond, or loan guarantee. If "Yes," provide details, including date, name and address of Lender, FHA or VA case number, if any, and reasons for the action.)	☐	☐	☐	☐
f. Are you presently delinquent or in default on any Federal debt or any other loan, mortgage, financial obligation, bond, or loan guarantee? If "Yes," give details as described in the preceding question.	☐	☐	☐	☐
g. Are you obligated to pay alimony, child support, or separate maintenance?	☐	☐	☐	☐
h. Is any part of the down payment borrowed?	☐	☐	☐	☐
i. Are you a co-maker or endorser on a note?	☐	☐	☐	☐
j. Are you a U.S. citizen?	☐	☐	☐	☐
k. Are you a permanent resident alien?	☐	☐	☐	☐
l. Do you intend to occupy the property as your primary residence? If "Yes," complete question m below.	☐	☐	☐	☐
m. Have you had an ownership interest in a property in the last three years?	☐	☐	☐	☐
(1) What type of property did you own—principal residence (PR), second home (SH), or investment property (IP)?				
(2) How did you hold title to the home—solely by yourself (S), jointly with your spouse (SP), or jointly with another person (O)?				

IX. ACKNOWLEDGMENT AND AGREEMENT

Each of the undersigned specifically represents to Lender and to Lender's actual or potential agents, brokers, processors, attorneys, insurers, servicers, successors and assigns and agrees and acknowledges that: (1) the information provided in this application is true and correct as of the date set forth opposite my signature and that any intentional or negligent misrepresentation of this information contained in this application may result in civil liability, including monetary damages, to any person who may suffer any loss due to reliance upon any misrepresentation that I have made on this application, and/or in criminal penalties including, but not limited to, fine or imprisonment or both under the provisions of Title 18, United States Code, Sec. 1001, et seq.; (2) the loan requested pursuant to this application (the "Loan") will be secured by a mortgage or deed of trust on the property described herein; (3) the property will not be used for any illegal or prohibited purpose or use; (4) all statements made in this application are made for the purpose of obtaining a residential mortgage loan; (5) the property will be occupied as indicated herein; (6) any owner or servicer of the Loan may verify any information contained in the application from any source named in this application, and Lender, its successors or assigns may retain the original and/or an electronic record of this application, even if the Loan is not approved; (7) the Lender and its agents, brokers, insurers, servicers, successors and assigns may continuously rely on the information contained in the application, and I am obligated to amend and/or supplement the information provided in this application if any of the material facts that I have represented herein should change prior to closing of the Loan; (8) in the event that my payments on the Loan become delinquent, the owner or servicer of the Loan may, in addition to any other rights and remedies that it may have relating to such delinquency, report my name and account information to one or more consumer credit reporting agencies; (9) ownership of the Loan and/or administration of the Loan account may be transferred with such notice as may be required by law; (10) neither Lender nor its agents, brokers, insurers, servicers, successors or assigns has made any representation or warranty, express or implied, to me regarding the property or the condition or value of the property; and (11) my transmission of this application as an "electronic record" containing my "electronic signature," as those terms are defined in applicable federal and/or state laws (excluding audio and video recordings), or my facsimile transmission of this application containing a facsimile of my signature, shall be as effective, enforceable and valid as if a paper version of this application were delivered containing my original written signature.

Borrower's Signature	Date	Co-Borrower's Signature	Date
X		X	

X. INFORMATION FOR GOVERNMENT MONITORING PURPOSES

The following information is requested by the Federal Government for certain types of loans related to a dwelling in order to monitor the lender's compliance with equal credit opportunity, fair housing and home mortgage disclosure laws. You are not required to furnish this information, but are encouraged to do so. The law provides that a lender may discriminate neither on the basis of this information, nor on whether you choose to furnish it. If you furnish the information, please provide both ethnicity and race. For race, you may check more than one designation. If you do not furnish ethnicity, race, or sex, under Federal regulations, this lender is required to note the information on the basis of visual observation or surname. If you do not wish to furnish the information, please check the box below. (Lender must review the above material to assure that the disclosures satisfy all requirements to which the lender is subject under applicable state law for the particular type of loan applied for.)

BORROWER	☐ I do not wish to furnish this information.		CO-BORROWER	☐ I do not wish to furnish this information.	
Ethnicity:	☐ Hispanic or Latino	☐ Not Hispanic or Latino	**Ethnicity:**	☐ Hispanic or Latino	☐ Not Hispanic or Latino
Race:	☐ American Indian or Alaska Native	☐ Asian ☐ Black or African American	**Race:**	☐ American Indian or Alaska Native	☐ Asian ☐ Black or African American
	☐ Native Hawaiian or Other Pacific Islander	☐ White		☐ Native Hawaiian or Other Pacific Islander	☐ White
Sex:	☐ Female	☐ Male	**Sex:**	☐ Female	☐ Male

To be Completed by Interviewer	Interviewer's Name (print or type)		Name and Address of Interviewer's Employer
This application was taken by: ☐ Face-to-face interview ☐ Mail ☐ Telephone ☐ Internet	Interviewer's Signature	Date	
	Interviewer's Phone Number (incl. area code)		

FIGURE 9.1   Uniform Residential Loan Application.

127

Continuation Sheet/Residential Loan Application

Use this continuation sheet if you need more space to complete the Residential Loan Application. Mark B for Borrower or C for Co-Borrower.	Borrower:	Agency Case Number:
	Co-Borrower:	Lender Case Number:

I/We fully understand that it is a Federal crime punishable by fine or imprisonment, or both, to knowingly make any false statements concerning any of the above facts as applicable under the provisions of Title 18, United States Code, Section 1001, et seq.

Borrower's Signature	Date	Co-Borrower's Signature	Date
X		X	

FIGURE 9.1 Uniform Residential Loan Application

balance sheet and a year-to-date profit and loss statement. If you are involved in other types of partnerships that are "pass-through" entities (sub-chapter-S corporation, limited-liability company, limited partnership), include your tax schedule K-1 from these.

Something your lender might not specifically request (but that I recommend nonetheless) is a personal financial statement. This details all of your assets, liabilities, income, and expenses. It's very much like a business financial statement—except it's personal.

The 1003 application form allows you to provide some of this information (in tiny, often too-few boxes), which is why the lender might not routinely ask for more. So why provide it? As they say in upscale restaurants, it's all in the presentation. Giving the lender a personal financial statement accomplishes a couple of worthwhile objectives. It allows you to provide greater detail in a more readable format. What if you have several sources of income, own several properties, are involved in a number of partnerships? It allows you to clarify what might be left unclear on the FNMA form. It also announces that you have a good grip on your financial circumstances and have the acumen to present those circumstances in a professional manner.

Born of my own need to provide this kind of information frequently, I developed an Excel®-based software package to automate the process, one that we now sell (called, oddly enough, *Personal Financial Statement*) at realdata.com. The model allows a user to enter a considerable amount of information, including details on properties that he or she might own entirely or in a partnership (less than 100 percent). The program does the math, so the balance sheet always balances and prints out a document with a very professional appearance.

These sample pages shown in Figure 9.2 will give you an idea of some of the information you might include in a personal financial statement.

There is a side-benefit to maintaining your personal financial statement in a software program and in fact that benefit is the main reason I wrote the program originally for my own use: It is not uncommon for commercial lenders to require a borrower to provide an updated statement each year, even after the loan is closed. Lending is all about risk, and the lender is looking for assurance that the borrower remains sound—or, if you're a glass-half-empty sort of person, that the borrower has not become overextended. Completing such a form from scratch each year used to take me the

Personal Financial Statement
Vs 4.2 Build 1.1 Copyright © 1997-2003 RealData® Inc

Applicant: **Joseph Byer**

Co-applicant: **Mary Byer**

Assets	Applicant	Co-Applicant	Liabilities & Net Worth	Applicant	Co-Applicant
Cash in Checking & Savings (1):	34,400	15,460	Loans / Notes Payable (6):	31,000	0
Cash in Property Accounts:	0	0	Accounts & Bills Payable (6):	0	0
Cash in IRAs (1):	6,475	4,750	Due to Brokers:	0	0
Marketable Securities (5)	1,544	0	Real Estate Mortgages (3):	156,700	242,200
Marketable Securities, IRA (5):	6,450	5,785	Unpaid Tax (Including Income & RE):	0	0
Life Insurance - CSV:	8,000	3,000	Other Debts:	0	0
Real Estate Owned (100%) (3):	500,000	400,000	Bal. Due on Partnerships, Notes (4):	0	0
R.E. Owned (Less than 100%) (3):	0	0	**TOTAL LIABILITIES:**	**187,700**	**242,200**
Partnerships/PC Interests (4):	10,000	0	**NET WORTH:**	**451,169**	**221,795**
Personal Property:	50,000	35,000	**TOTAL LIAB. & NET WORTH:**	**638,869**	**463,995**
Other Assets	0	0			
Automobiles/Vehicles (incl. boats):	0	0			
Notes Receivable (2):	22,000	0			
Accounts Receivable (2)	0	0			
Non-Readily Marketable Sec. (5):	0	0			
Non-Readily Marketable Sec., IRA (5):	0	0			
TOTAL ASSETS:	**638,869**	**463,995**			

Annual Income	Applicant	Co-Applicant	Annual Expenditures	Applicant	Co-Applicant
Salary or Adjusted Gross Income.	38,500	49,500	Federal Income & Other Taxes:	12,931	9,900
Bonus or Commissions:	19,750	0	State Income & Other Taxes:	2,351	0
Dividends and Interest:	525	0	Property Taxes (3):	5,450	4,800
Net Real Estate Income (3):	0	45,600	Mortgage Payments (3):	12,321	20,119
Capital Gains.	0	0	Property Insurance (3):	1,250	1,800
Other Income.	0	0	Life Insurance:	625	540
TOTAL INCOME:	**58,775**	**95,100**	Rental / Condominium Fees:	0	0
			Interest & Principal on Loans/Bills (6):	3,120	0
			Investments:	0	0
			Alimony / Child Support:	0	0
			Tuition Expense:	0	0
			Medical Expenses:	5,000	0
			Other Expenses:	0	0
			TOTAL EXPENDITURES:	**43,047**	**37,159**

Notes: Net Real Estate Income is before debt service, it is also before property taxes and insurance, which are accounted for under Annual Expenditures.
The assets, liabilities, income, mortgage payments and insurance of property owned at less than 100% are reported here factored by the percentage owned.

Contingent Liabilities	YES	NO
Are you a guarantor, co-maker, or endorser for any debt of an individual, corporation, or partnership?	☐	☑
Do you have any outstanding letters of credit or surety bonds?	☐	☑
Are there any suits or legal actions pending against you?	☐	☑
Are you contingently liable on any lease or contract?	☐	☑

FIGURE 9.2   Personal Financial Statement (page 1 of 7).

Personal Information			
Applicant		**Co-applicant**	
Name:	Joseph Byer	Name:	Mary Byer
Employer:	Classic Homes Realty	Employer:	Pioneer Automotive
Employer Street Address:	222 Madison St.	Employer Street Address:	56 Lexington Rd.
City, State, ZIP:	South Haven, CT 06999	City, State, ZIP:	South Haven, CT 06999
Employer Phone Number:	203-555-1213	Employer Phone Number:	203-555-9978
No. of Years with Employer:	10	No. of Years with Employer:	8
Title/Position:	Sales Associate	Title/Position:	Office Manager
Name of Prev. Employer:		Name of Prev. Employer:	South Haven Construction
Position at Prev. Employer:		Position at Prev. Employer:	Office Manager
No. of Years w/ Prev. Emp.:		No. of Years w/ Prev. Emp.:	2
Home Street Address:	758 Summer St.	Home Street Address:	758 Summer St.
City, State, ZIP:	South Haven, CT 06999	City, State, ZIP:	South Haven, CT 06999
Home Phone:	203-555-9999	Home Phone:	203-555-9999
Social Security Number:	999-88-9999	Social Security Number:	999-99-8888
Date of Birth:	08/01/68	Date of Birth:	10/10/72
Inc. Tax returns filed through:	2003	Inc. Tax returns filed through:	2003
Any returns being audited?	No	Any returns being audited?	No
If yes, what year(s)?		If yes, what year(s)?	
Any taxes past due?	No	Any taxes past due?	No
If yes, amount:		If yes, amount:	
Ever declared bankruptcy?	No	Ever declared bankruptcy?	No
Have you drawn a will?	Yes	Have you drawn a will?	Yes
Year drawn:	1999	Year drawn:	1999
Name of executor:	John Marshall, Esq.	Name of executor:	John Marshall, Esq.
Number of dependents:	2	Number of dependents:	2
Do you have financial plan?	Yes	Do you have financial plan?	Yes
If yes, name of planner:	Alex Hamilton, CFP	If yes, name of planner:	Alex Hamilton, CFP
Life Insurance - CSV:	$8,000	Life Insurance - CSV:	$3,000
Name of Insured:	Joseph Byer	Name of Insured:	Mary Byer
Name of Company:	Vitabreva Insurance	Name of Company:	Vitabreva Insurance
Policy Number:	99-55-77-88	Policy Number:	92-65-87-99
Beneficiary:	Mary Byer	Beneficiary:	Joseph Byer

FIGURE 9.2   Personal Financial Statement (page 2 of 7).

Schedule 1: Cash in Checking & Savings Accounts

	Applicant		Co-applicant

Checking Account #1

Bank Name:	First American Federal S & L
Street Address:	101 Orange St
City, State ZIP:	South Haven, CT 06999
Checking Account #:	684545-987211
Amount:	$6,400

Checking Account #2

Bank Name:	(Joint account with applicant)
Street Address:	
City, State ZIP:	
Checking Account #:	
Amount:	

Checking Account #3

Bank Name:	
Street Address:	
City, State ZIP:	
Checking Account #:	
Amount:	

Checking Account #4

Bank Name:	
Street Address:	
City, State ZIP:	
Checking Account #:	
Amount:	

Checking Account #5

Bank Name:	
Street Address:	
City, State ZIP:	
Checking Account #:	
Amount:	

Checking Account #6

Bank Name:	
Street Address:	
City, State ZIP:	
Checking Account #:	
Amount:	

Checking Account #7

Bank Name:	
Street Address:	
City, State ZIP:	
Checking Account #:	
Amount:	

Checking Account #8

Bank Name:	
Street Address:	
City, State ZIP:	
Checking Account #:	
Amount:	

Checking Account #9

Bank Name:	
Street Address:	
City, State ZIP:	
Checking Account #:	
Amount:	

Checking Account #10

Bank Name:	
Street Address:	
City, State ZIP:	
Checking Account #:	
Amount:	

Savings Account #1

Bank Name:	First American Federal S & L
Street Address:	101 Orange St
City, State ZIP:	South Haven, CT 06999
Savings Account #:	99-78994554
Amount:	$24,500

Savings Account #2

Bank Name:	S. H. Auto Dealers Federal Credit Union
Street Address:	205 Orange St.
City, State ZIP:	South Haven, CT 06999
Savings Account #:	A77789444
Amount:	$15,460

Savings Account #3

Bank Name:	Vesuvius Money Market Fund
Street Address:	P. O. Box 111
City, State ZIP:	Marina del Tuna, CA 99999
Savings Account #:	VT098708172399937 ☐ IRA
Amount:	$3,500

Savings Account #4

Bank Name:	Vesuvius Certificate of Deposit
Street Address:	P. O. Box 111
City, State ZIP:	Marina del Tuna, CA 99999
Savings Account #:	IRA98765576578 ☑ IRA
Amount:	$4,750

Savings Account #5

Bank Name:	Vesuvius Certificate of Deposit
Street Address:	P. O. Box 111
City, State ZIP:	Marina del Tuna, CA 99999
Savings Account #:	IRA8913568528 ☑ IRA
Amount:	$6,475

Savings Account #6

Bank Name:	
Street Address:	
City, State ZIP:	
Savings Account #:	☐ IRA
Amount:	

Savings Account #7

Bank Name:	
Street Address:	
City, State ZIP:	
Savings Account #:	☐ IRA
Amount:	

Savings Account #8

Bank Name:	
Street Address:	
City, State ZIP:	
Savings Account #:	☐ IRA
Amount:	

Savings Account #9

Bank Name:	
Street Address:	
City, State ZIP:	
Savings Account #:	☐ IRA
Amount:	

Savings Account #10

Bank Name:	
Street Address:	
City, State ZIP:	
Savings Account #:	☐ IRA
Amount:	

FIGURE 9.2   Personal Financial Statement (page 3 of 7).

Schedule 2: Notes and Accounts Receivable			
	Applicant		**Co-applicant**
Notes Receivable #1	List Name & Address of Maker	**Notes Receivable #2**	List Name & Address of Maker
Name of Maker:	Bernard Byer	Name of Maker:	
Street Address:	1202 West Morgan Ave	Street Address:	
City, State, ZIP:	Burrville, NV 78888	City, State, ZIP:	
Amount:	$14,000	Amount:	
Notes Receivable #3		**Notes Receivable #4**	
Name of Maker:	Lenore Byer	Name of Maker:	
Street Address:	1202 West Morgan Ave	Street Address:	
City, State, ZIP:	Burrville, NV 78888	City, State, ZIP:	
Amount:	$8,000	Amount:	
Notes Receivable #5		**Notes Receivable #6**	
Name of Maker:		Name of Maker:	
Street Address:		Street Address:	
City, State, ZIP:		City, State, ZIP:	
Amount:		Amount:	
Notes Receivable #7		**Notes Receivable #8**	
Name of Maker:		Name of Maker:	
Street Address:		Street Address:	
City, State, ZIP:		City, State, ZIP:	
Amount:		Amount:	
Notes Receivable #9		**Notes Receivable #10**	
Name of Maker:		Name of Maker:	
Street Address:		Street Address:	
City, State, ZIP:		City, State, ZIP:	
Amount:		Amount:	
Notes Receivable #11		**Notes Receivable #12**	
Name of Maker:		Name of Maker:	
Street Address:		Street Address:	
City, State, ZIP:		City, State, ZIP:	
Amount:		Amount:	

Accounts Receivable #1	List Name & Address of Maker	**Accounts Receivable #2**	List Name & Address of Maker
Name of Maker:		Name of Maker:	
Street Address:		Street Address:	
City, State, ZIP:		City, State, ZIP:	
Amount:		Amount:	
Accounts Receivable #3		**Accounts Receivable #4**	
Name of Maker:		Name of Maker:	
Street Address:		Street Address:	
City, State, ZIP:		City, State, ZIP:	
Amount:		Amount:	
Accounts Receivable #5		**Accounts Receivable #6**	
Name of Maker:		Name of Maker:	
Street Address:		Street Address:	
City, State, ZIP:		City, State, ZIP:	
Amount:		Amount:	
Accounts Receivable #7		**Accounts Receivable #8**	
Name of Maker:		Name of Maker:	
Street Address:		Street Address:	
City, State, ZIP:		City, State, ZIP:	
Amount:		Amount:	
Accounts Receivable #9		**Accounts Receivable #10**	
Name of Maker:		Name of Maker:	
Street Address:		Street Address:	
City, State, ZIP:		City, State, ZIP:	
Amount:		Amount:	
Accounts Receivable #11		**Accounts Receivable #12**	
Name of Maker:		Name of Maker:	
Street Address:		Street Address:	
City, State, ZIP:		City, State, ZIP:	
Amount:		Amount:	

FIGURE 9.2   Personal Financial Statement (page 4 of 7).

Schedule 3: Real Estate (Personal Residence, Real Estate Investments & Mortgage Debt)		
Applicant		**Co-applicant**
100% Owned (Property #1)	**100% Owned (Property #2)**	
Type of Property: Duplex - owner occupied	Type of Property:	
Street Address: 818 Commonage Road	Street Address:	
City, State, ZIP: Yuma, AZ 85364	City, State, ZIP:	
Legal Owner(s): David Caswell	Legal Owner(s):	
Miriam Caswell		
Purchase Price: $85,500	Purchase Price:	
Date of Purch. (mm/dd/yy): 1/15/98	Date of Purch. (mm/dd/yy):	
Current Market Value: $89,500	Current Market Value:	
Mortgage Holder: Bank of the Americas	Mortgage Holder:	
Loan Number: 45-78451-584-55	Loan Number:	
Mortgage Amt. Outstanding: $81,995	Mortgage Amt. Outstanding:	
Monthly Payment: $524.00	Monthly Payment:	
Interest Rate: 6.500%	Interest Rate:	
Annual Taxes: $425	Annual Taxes:	
Annual Insurance: $750	Annual Insurance:	
Annual Gross Income: $3,600	Annual Gross Income:	
Annual Net Op. Income: $2,425	Annual Net Op. Income:	
Property Cash in Accounts: $1,500	Property Cash in Accounts:	
100% Owned (Property #3)	**100% Owned (Property #4)**	
Type of Property:	Type of Property:	
Street Address:	Street Address:	
City, State, ZIP:	City, State, ZIP:	
Legal Owner(s):	Legal Owner(s):	
Purchase Price:	Purchase Price:	
Date of Purch. (mm/dd/yy):	Date of Purch. (mm/dd/yy):	
Current Market Value:	Current Market Value:	
Mortgage Holder:	Mortgage Holder:	
Loan Number:	Loan Number:	
Mortgage Amt. Outstanding:	Mortgage Amt. Outstanding:	
Monthly Payment:	Monthly Payment:	
Interest Rate:	Interest Rate:	
Annual Taxes:	Annual Taxes:	
Annual Insurance:	Annual Insurance:	
Annual Gross Income:	Annual Gross Income:	
Annual Net Op. Income:	Annual Net Op. Income:	
Property Cash in Accounts:	Property Cash in Accounts:	
Less Than 100% Owned (Property #5)	**Less Than 100% Owned (Property #6)**	
Type of Property:	Type of Property: Multi-Family (6 unit)	
Street Address:	Street Address: 10 Gallowtree Gate	
City, State, ZIP:	City, State, ZIP: Manchester, NH 85602	
Percentage of Ownership:	Percentage of Ownership: 33.00%	
Legal Owner(s):	Legal Owner(s): Jack King	
	Miriam Caswell	
Purchase Price:	Purchase Price: $299,000	
Date of Purch. (mm/dd/yy):	Date of Purch. (mm/dd/yy): 4/15/96	
Current Market Value:	Current Market Value: $318,000	
Mortgage Holder:	Mortgage Holder: Grafton Savings and Loan	
Loan Number:	Loan Number: 148-567-5284	
Mortgage Amt. Outstanding:	Mortgage Amt. Outstanding: $240,395	
Monthly Payment:	Monthly Payment: $1,612.00	
Interest Rate:	Interest Rate: 71.250%	
Annual Taxes:	Annual Taxes: $3,590	
Annual Insurance:	Annual Insurance: $1,852	
Annual Gross Income:	Annual Gross Income: $48,600	
Annual Net Op. Income:	Annual Net Op. Income: $34,500	
Property Cash in Accounts:	Property Cash in Accounts: $65,000	

FIGURE 9.2   Personal Financial Statement (page 5 of 7).

Schedule 4: Partnerships (Business/Professional & Investments)

Business / Professional	Applicant	Business / Professional	Co-applicant
Name:		Name:	
Date of Initial Investment:		Date of Initial Investment:	
Cost:		Cost:	
Percent Owned:		Percent Owned:	
Current Market Value:		Current Market Value:	
Bal. Due on Partnerships:		Bal. Due on Partnerships:	
Final Contribution Date:		Final Contribution Date:	

Business / Professional		Business / Professional	
Name:		Name:	
Date of Initial Investment:		Date of Initial Investment:	
Cost:		Cost:	
Percent Owned:		Percent Owned:	
Current Market Value:		Current Market Value:	
Bal. Due on Partnerships:		Bal. Due on Partnerships:	
Final Contribution Date:		Final Contribution Date:	

Investments (Including Tax Shelters)		Investments (Including Tax Shelters)	
Name:	Loft Limited Partnership	Name:	
Date of Initial Investment:	8/28/2003	Date of Initial Investment:	
Cost:	$10,000	Cost:	
Percent Owned:	3.000%	Percent Owned:	
Current Market Value:	$10,000	Current Market Value:	
Bal. Due on Partnerships:	$0	Bal. Due on Partnerships:	
Final Contribution Date:		Final Contribution Date:	

Investments (Including Tax Shelters)		Investments (Including Tax Shelters)	
Name:		Name:	
Date of Initial Investment:		Date of Initial Investment:	
Cost:		Cost:	
Percent Owned:		Percent Owned:	
Current Market Value:		Current Market Value:	
Bal. Due on Partnerships:		Bal. Due on Partnerships:	
Final Contribution Date:		Final Contribution Date:	

Schedule 5: All Securities (Including all mutual funds)

Readily Marketable Securities	Applicant	Readily Marketable Securities	Co-applicant
No. of Shares/Face Value:	298.22	No. of Shares/Face Value:	175.82
Description:	Growth & Income Fund ☑ IRA	Description:	Growth & Income Fund ☑ IRA
Cost:	$4,800	Cost:	$3,600
Current Market Value:	$6,450	Current Market Value:	$5,785
Pledged:	☐ Yes ☑ No	Pledged:	☐ Yes ☑ No

Readily Marketable Securities		Readily Marketable Securities	
No. of Shares/Face Value:	2866	No. of Shares/Face Value:	
Description:	Penny Stocks ☐ IRA	Description:	☐ IRA
Cost:	$684	Cost:	
Current Market Value:	$1,544	Current Market Value:	
Pledged:	☐ Yes ☑ No	Pledged:	☐ Yes ☑ No

Non-Readily Marketable Securities		Non-Readily Marketable Securities	
No. of Shares/Face Value:		No. of Shares/Face Value:	
Description:	☐ IRA	Description:	☐ IRA
Cost:		Cost:	
Current Market Value:		Current Market Value:	
Pledged:	☐ Yes ☐ No	Pledged:	☐ Yes ☐ No

Non-Readily Marketable Securities		Non-Readily Marketable Securities	
No. of Shares/Face Value:		No. of Shares/Face Value:	
Description:		Description:	☐ IRA
Cost:	☐ IRA	Cost:	
Current Market Value:		Current Market Value:	
Pledged:	☐ Yes ☐ No	Pledged:	☐ Yes ☐ No

FIGURE 9.2   Personal Financial Statement (page 6 of 7).

Schedule 6: Notes & Accounts Payable

Applicant		Co-applicant	
Enter Notes Payable Below (Including Installment Notes, Equity Lines/Loans, and Credit Cards)			
Due To:	MasterBlaster	Due To:	
Type of Facility:	Credit Card	Type of Facility:	
Amount of Line:	$10,000	Amount of Line:	
Collateral:		Collateral:	
Interest Rate:	21.000%	Interest Rate:	
Maturity:	revolving	Maturity:	
Monthly Payment:	$150.00	Monthly Payment:	
Balance Outstanding:	$1,000	Balance Outstanding:	
Enter Notes Payable Below (Including Installment Notes, Equity Lines/Loans, and Credit Cards)			
Due To:	South Haven Equity Assoc.	Due To:	
Type of Facility:	HELOC	Type of Facility:	
Amount of Line:	$50,000	Amount of Line:	
Collateral:	758 Summer St.	Collateral:	
Interest Rate:	4.250%	Interest Rate:	
Maturity:	7/2/2010	Maturity:	
Monthly Payment:	$110.00	Monthly Payment:	
Balance Outstanding:	$30,000	Balance Outstanding:	
Enter Notes Payable Below (Including Installment Notes, Equity Lines/Loans, and Credit Cards)			
Due To:		Due To:	
Type of Facility:		Type of Facility:	
Amount of Line:		Amount of Line:	
Collateral:		Collateral:	
Interest Rate:		Interest Rate:	
Maturity:		Maturity:	
Monthly Payment:		Monthly Payment:	
Balance Outstanding:		Balance Outstanding:	
Enter Accounts and Bills Payable			
Due To:		Due To:	
Type of Facility:		Type of Facility:	
Amount of Line:		Amount of Line:	
Collateral:		Collateral:	
Interest Rate:		Interest Rate:	
Maturity:		Maturity:	
Monthly Payment:		Monthly Payment:	
Balance Outstanding:		Balance Outstanding:	

I/we have provided this information for the purpose of obtaining or maintaining credit for myself or on behalf of a corporation, partnership or other business entity with which I am associated, or as a guarantor for another person or business entity. I/we certify that this is a true, complete, and accurate statement of my/our financial condition as of 10/10/2004. I/we agree that the accuracy of this financial statement may be verified to determine my/our creditworthiness.

Applicant: _____   Date:
       Joseph Byer

Co-Applicant: _____   Date:
       Mary Byer

FIGURE 9.2   **Personal Financial Statement (page 7 of 7).**

better part of a day (can somebody please help me find the loan numbers and terms on those five mortgages?). With the automated form, I just update whatever has changed since I used it last.

> **Rule of Thumb:** *Even if you don't choose to maintain an automated version of your personal financial statement, get a blank form from a commercial bank, make copies, fill one out, and update it periodically. It's useful for helping you keep an eye on your general financial picture; and when you really do need to supply this information as part of a loan application, you won't need to scramble looking for the information.*

About the Property

The property will stand as security for the mortgage loan, so information about the property is key to your success in borrowing money. At the very top of the pile of papers you'll call your "loan package," put the purchase contract. It identifies the property and the parties involved and describes the terms of the deal—price, proposed financing, contingencies, timing, special conditions, etc.

> **Rule of Thumb:** *Whether you are a buyer or a seller, have an attorney who specializes in real estate scrutinize the contract before you affix your signature. Don't misinterpret this as generic "eat your vegetables, they're good for you" kind of advice that any intelligent grownup can feel free to ignore. It's tempting to assume, just because the contract is written in apparent English and seems to mean what it says, that you fully understand its implications. There are terms of art whose presence—or absence—can prove crucial. Resist that temptation and engage a good attorney.*

You should also provide the lender with copies of the leases or with estoppel certificates. With residential properties, leases should suffice. If this is a commercial building, you'll probably need to ask the seller to procure estoppels from the lessees.

With small residential properties—four units or less—give the lender a rent roll showing current and expected future rents for each unit. Have another copy ready to give to the person who is performing the appraisal. It is also a good idea to prepare an Annual Property Operating Data (APOD) form and to have the ready if needed. As I discussed earlier, the underwriting for a small residential investment is similar to that for a personal residence except that the lender will typically count 75 percent of the rent and add it to your personal income before applying the "front" and "back" ratios. A more detailed financial analysis of the property is an important part of your own decision-making process, but it probably won't gain you much traction with the lender.

On the other hand, if the property is commercial or if it's more than four units of residential, then it can be very worthwhile to prepare a presentation that includes pro-forma projections of cash flows, potential resale, ratios such as DCR, rates of return, and other key metrics.

An approach we take in our software is to present the results of our financial analysis in a variety of ways. One is quite detailed. It's useful for you as the investor, especially as you're trying to shape the deal: "Now how does it look if I can get the second mortgage at 7 percent instead of 8 percent?" A second type of report (we call it a "cash flow and resale summary") still provides a great deal of information but is not so granular in its detail. Yet another is designed as a presentation. It captures the essentials and displays them in a way that makes them easy to apprehend. This is the sort of presentation that can be effective in conveying the deal's essentials to a lender or partner. You can still provide the detailed version as a backup if needed, to answer questions like, "So, where'd you get *that* number?" A final format is a simple "executive summary."

On the following pages you'll see some examples. Figure 9.3 shows the initial 10 years' projections in a cash flow and resale summary. It provides a great deal of information, but aggregates the depreciation and amortization as well as the financing details for multiple mortgages. Following that is Figure 9.4, one sample page extracted from a presentation we call our "Real Estate Business Plan." This style of report is best for an initial presentation to a lender or client because it focuses on essential information and presents it thematically—a page about sources and uses of funds, another about financing, yet another about gross income and total expenses, etc. The page I've chosen to show here is one that displays the key metrics, items of particular interest to a lender. Figure 9.5 is an executive summary, just the basic facts about the property's expected performance in the first year.

Cash Flow and Resale Summary Report - Years 1-10
The RealData Building

	2004	2005	2006	2007	2008	2009	2010	2011	2012	2013
GROSS INCOME	153,458	187,546	199,343	208,944	217,228	221,829	224,910	227,380	231,714	233,796
- Vacancy & Credit Allowance	4,604	5,626	5,980	6,208	6,517	6,655	6,747	6,821	6,961	7,014
- Operating Expenses	34,121	43,796	45,439	46,960	48,627	50,118	51,594	53,063	54,713	56,286
NET OPERATING INCOME	114,734	138,123	147,924	153,775	162,084	165,056	166,568	167,465	170,049	170,496
- Interest, All Loans	56,982	66,530	70,405	69,070	67,841	66,920	76,337	75,970	75,459	73,790
- Depreciation and Amortization	17,207	21,898	25,824	28,391	31,907	38,963	27,571	26,710	28,710	24,615
+ Interest, Funded Reserves	3,333	2,089	3,109	2,121	2,206	2,294	2,306	2,481	2,560	2,834
INCOME OR (LOSS)	43,897	53,684	54,804	53,435	64,801	62,477	53,046	66,267	70,461	74,764
(LOSS) UTILIZED THIS YEAR	0	0	0	0	0	0	0	0	0	0
TAXABLE INCOME	43,897	53,684	54,804	58,435	64,801	62,477	53,046	66,267	70,461	74,764
NET OPERATING INCOME	114,734	138,123	147,924	153,775	162,084	166,096	166,568	167,465	170,049	170,496
- Debt Service, All Mortgages	140,342	103,289	61,938	81,938	81,938	81,938	91,397	91,397	91,397	91,397
+ Proceeds of Refinance	213,090	0	0	0	0	0	200,163	0	0	0
- Capital Expenditures and Funded Reserves*	(28,608)	8,060	93,787	46,240	10,473	8	5,000	0	0	0
CASH FLOW BEFORE TAXES	(28,608)	41,835	(27,801)	25,598	69,674	83,118	270,334	78,068	78,652	79,080
Reserves Utilized	28,608	0	27,801	0	0	0	0	0	0	0
Reserves Remaining	74,725	77,714	53,022	55,143	57,348	59,642	62,028	64,509	57,089	69,773
NET CASH FLOW AFTER UTILIZING RESERVES	0	41,635	0	25,598	69,674	93,118	270,334	76,060	70,652	79,089
- Income Tax Attributable to Property	13,608	16,942	16,069	16,115	20,088	19,368	19,544	20,543	21,843	23,177
CASH FLOW AFTER TAXES AND RESERVES	(13,608)	25,192	(16,969)	7,483	49,585	63,750	250,790	55,525	56,809	55,912
GAIN OR (LOSS) ON SALE, Real Estate	7,998	24,958	40,945	72,269	163,693	212,360	244,955	276,110	322,115	349,521
GAIN ON SALE, Personal Property	0	0	0	0	0	0	0	0	0	0
PROJECTED SELLING PRICE, incl. personal prop.	1,197,000	1,201,000	1,286,000	1,337,000	1,409,000	1,435,000	1,448,000	1,458,000	1,479,000	1,462,000
- Costs of Sale	83,790	84,070	90,020	93,590	98,630	100,450	101,360	101,920	103,530	103,740
- Mortgage Payoffs	566,620	643,862	632,329	619,461	605,105	589,067	776,190	701,782	745,824	728,216
+ Balance of Reserve Fund	74,725	77,714	53,022	56,143	57,348	59,942	62,028	64,509	67,089	69,773
BEFORE-TAX SALE PROCEEDS	521,315	550,782	616,673	679,091	762,613	805,105	632,478	666,827	696,736	719,816
- Total Federal Tax on Sale	(1,124)	2,853	5,331	12,622	31,770	46,621	53,968	82,111	72,764	79,420
AFTER-TAX SALE PROCEEDS	522,439	547,929	611,342	666,469	730,843	759,484	578,510	584,716	623,972	640,397
Internal Rate of Return, Before Tax	8.35%	11.00%	11.30%	12.01%	13.93%	14.30%	14.04%	14.18%	14.43%	14.44%
Modified Internal Rate of Return, Before Tax	8.39%	11.00%	11.20%	11.84%	13.62%	13.84%	13.42%	13.22%	13.15%	12.90%
Internal Rate of Return, After-Tax	5.22%	7.47%	7.90%	8.41%	10.09%	10.48%	10.32%	10.49%	10.76%	10.81%
Modified Internal Rate of Return, After-Tax	5.22%	7.42%	7.75%	8.25%	9.67%	10.23%	10.02%	10.04%	10.15%	10.07%
PV, Net Operating Income & Reversion	1,126,928	1,942,666	1,218,791	1,254,670	1,319,427	1,343,537	1,356,882	1,370,660	1,387,111	1,394,860
PV, CFAT and Sale Proceeds after Taxes	455,954	450,321	440,321	437,288	461,368	467,803	461,191	464,704	472,775	474,078
EQUITY, excluding reserves	530,360	557,138	553,671	717,539	603,865	845,913	671,810	694,238	733,176	753,784
RETURN ON EQUITY (CFBT/Equity)	-5.47%	7.51%	-4.25%	3.57%	8.67%	9.83%	10.45%	10.99%	19.73%	10.49%

FIGURE 9.3   Cash Flow and Resale Summary Report.

Resale and Rates of Return

Resale at End of 2023

Projected Selling Price:	$1,466,000
Cost of Sale:	$102,620
Gain (Loss) on Sale:	$580,795
Federal Tax on Sale:	$138,280
Before-Tax Sale Proceeds:	$1,055,536
After-Tax Sale Proceeds:	$917,256

Measures of Investment Quality

IRR, Before-Tax:	14.18%
IRR, After-Tax:	10.78%
MIRR, Before-Tax:	11.04%
MIRR, After Tax:	9.23%
PV, at 11.00%	$1,430,685

	Debt Coverage Ratio	Cap. Rate	Gross Income Multiplier	Cash on Cash Return	Operating Expense Ratio	Gross Income, $/sf	Operating Expenses, $/sf
2004	0.82	12.37%	6.70	-7.14%	22.23%	18.42	4.09
2005	1.34	12.32%	6.60	8.70%	23.35%	18.75	4.38
2006	1.81	12.26%	6.65	-5.78%	22.79%	19.93	4.54
2007	1.88	12.33%	6.66	5.32%	22.69%	20.69	4.70
2008	1.98	13.00%	6.69	14.49%	22.39%	21.72	4.86
2009	2.01	13.24%	6.67	17.28%	22.59%	22.18	5.01
2010	1.82	13.30%	6.64	56.20%	22.94%	22.49	5.16
2011	1.83	13.38%	6.60	15.81%	23.35%	22.74	5.31
2012	1.86	13.58%	6.58	16.35%	23.61%	23.17	5.47
2013	1.87	13.62%	6.53	16.44%	24.08%	23.38	5.63
2014	1.86	13.61%	6.49	16.42%	24.61%	23.53	5.79
2015	1.86	13.60%	6.44	16.39%	25.15%	23.69	5.96
2016	1.86	13.59%	6.39	16.36%	25.70%	23.86	6.13
2017	1.86	13.57%	6.34	16.33%	26.26%	24.03	6.31
2018	1.86	13.56%	6.29	16.30%	26.84%	24.20	6.49
2019	1.86	13.55%	6.24	16.26%	27.43%	24.38	6.69
2020	1.85	13.53%	6.18	16.21%	28.03%	24.56	6.88
2021	1.85	13.51%	6.13	16.17%	28.64%	24.75	7.09
2022	1.85	13.49%	6.07	16.12%	29.27%	24.94	7.30
2023	1.85	13.47%	6.01	16.06%	29.91%	25.14	7.52

FIGURE 9.4   Resale and Rates of Return.

Executive Summary
Year 1
Real Estate Investment Analysis

RealData Arms
691 Spring Street
South Haven, CT 06999

Prepared For:	Second National Bank 999 Main St South Haven, CT 06999	Prepared By:	RealData, Inc. P. O. Box 691 Southport, CT 06890
Property Type:	Apartment	Rentable Square Feet:	14,000

Report Prepared: March 1, 2004
Reporting Period: March - December 2004

Acquisition

Purchase Price, points & closing	669,564	47.83 per rsf
Capital Additions	10,000	
Cash Investment	174,100	25.62%
1st Mortgage	455,000	66.95% LTV
2d Mortgage	45,000	6.62% LTV

Income and Cash Flow

Gross Income	88,083
Vacancy & Credit Loss	2,642
Gross Operating Income	85,441
Operating Expenses	23,693
Net Operating Income	61,748
Total Interest	29,473
Depreciation and Amort.	14,845
Taxable Income	17,430
Debt Service	39,181
Cash Flow Before Taxes	22,567

Financial Measures

Capitalization Rate	11.23%
Debt Coverage Ratio	1.58
Internal Rate of Return	−22.05%
Present Value, at 11.50%	603,604
Gross Income Multiplier	6.28
Cash-on-Cash Return	15.55%
Gross Income per RSF	7.55
Operating Expense Ratio	26.90%
Operating Expenses per RSF	2.03

Note: If the period covered is a partial year, financial measures are annualized.

FIGURE 9.5   Executive Summary.

PART 3

THE OFFER, THE CLOSING, AND THEN WHAT?

10

What's Negotiable?

The answer is probably obvious: just about everything. Sometimes buyers and sellers get so wrapped up in the issue of price that they forget that the entire deal is an amalgam of gives and takes. When you have identified a property on which you want to make an offer, what issues would you expect to hammer out in your negotiations?

There are some contract items that descend on a stone tablet, items that are negotiable in name only. If financing is coming from a third-party lender (i.e., not the seller), then an engineering inspection and an environmental assessment—as well as an appraisal, of course—might not be open to discussion. But, most everything else is on the table. See the Contract Checklist.

Certainly not everything on this list will be appropriate to every deal. The purpose of the list is to help you avoid overlooking an item of importance. Also, there are other provisions that your attorney will include as a matter of course, such as pro-rating prepaid rental income and expenses.

The meaning of most of the items on this list should be clear, but several deserve some additional comment. A prespecified withdrawal date for your offer is not crucial, but you also don't want to leave an offer on the table indefinitely. The closing date and possession date will usually be the same. However if you're purchasing an owner-occupied property, the seller might need some extra time to vacate. You, on the other hand, might need to close quickly in order to keep your loan commitment and rate. You can close and allow the seller to hold over for a short time, paying you a per

Contract Checklist

_____ Price

_____ Amount of deposit

_____ Offer withdrawn if not accepted by (date)

_____ Inclusions (i.e., personal property)

_____ Closing date

_____ Possession date

_____ Seller's disclosure of known defects

_____ Seller's certification of accuracy of attached lease terms and operating expense
data

_____ Schedule of security deposits

_____ Structural inspection contingency

_____ Environmental survey contingency

_____ Buyer's access to property, documents, tenant records; amount of time for buyer's
due diligence

_____ Penalty for a default by buyer

_____ Penalty for a default by seller

_____ Financing contingency—third-party lender; amount and terms

_____ Financing from seller; amount and terms

_____ Seller's and Buyer's obligations in case of damage, destruction, or condemnation
prior to closing

_____ Guaranty by seller not to amend or enter into new lease agreements

_____ Guaranty by seller not to amend or enter into new service contracts

_____ Survival of warranties and representations

_____ Seller's rent guaranty in the event of vacancy before closing diem "use and occupancy" equal to your daily cost for mortgage, taxes, and insurance.

The seller should have already disclosed any known defects, but it is still prudent to attach these in writing to the contract. In regard to the inspection contingencies, the language should allow you to cancel the deal if anything is uncovered that in your sole judgment is sufficient cause to do so.

Earlier I devoted a good deal of discussion to the importance of financial and physical due diligence. The contract of sale is a good tool to pry information loose, so you should require access to the seller's property and tenant records as a condition of the purchase. Unless the property is large and complex, you should generally be able to deal with a 30-day period to satisfy this and the physical inspection contingencies—especially if you have the seller's cooperation in providing access to records.

The financing contingency is not necessary, of course, if you're paying all cash for the property. If that is the case, then you should replace it with an appraisal contingency. If an independent estimate of value shows that you are about to pay significantly more than the market price, then you have an escape hatch.

In regard to the penalty for buyer's default, you might discuss with your attorney whether to include liquidated damages as the seller's sole remedy. This means that you forfeit your deposit in the event of default but would not be liable for any additional amount. The alternative is to get tangled in a lawsuit for actual damages that the seller incurs due to your default. There is no cookie-cutter answer to which is best, so your best course is a) listen to the advice of your attorney regarding the contract language and b) don't default.

Any of a number of events could alter your deal-making landscape between the contract and the closing, and you should anticipate how to handle them. The property could be damaged, destroyed, or taken by eminent domain. Your attorney will probably recommend language that allows you a number of options you could exercise in the event of any of these occurrences. You definitely want to protect yourself against actions that the seller could take but that ultimately would be binding on you. To that end you want to be certain that the seller guarantees not to enter into new leases or service contracts or amend existing leases or contracts. Related to this promise is the last item on the checklist, survival of the warrantees and representations. Discuss with your attorney the exact language and length of time that makes sense for your situation. The seller might promise not to amend leases or contracts but then at the last moment, after you've completed your due diligence, do so anyway. You won't discover the deception until after the closing. This provision in the contract would make clear that you still have remedies against the seller even if you discover a misrepresentation or a violated warrantee after taking title to the property.

The last item on the checklist is not a legal issue but strictly a part of the deal that you might want to negotiate. Yet another event that could occur between contract and closing is the loss of one or more tenants on which you were relying for revenue when you formulated your offer. A concession you can ask from the seller is to guarantee the current rent roll. The way you might structure this is to identify the tenants and their rent amounts at the time of the contract; if any of those tenants should bolt before the closing, the seller would give you a credit for a specified number of months' rent to offset your loss while you look for a new tenant.

> **Rule of Thumb:** *Keep in mind that this is a bargaining chip, so you don't want to seek this concession unless it might have real value to you. For example, if the property is occupied by stable commercial tenants with long-term leases, then the chances of losing someone before the closing is probably minimal, as is the value of this concession. On the other hand, if there is a retail tenant teetering on the edge of insolvency or if the property is occupied by month-to-month residential tenants who could move out on short notice, then a clause like this could prevent sudden cash-flow shock.*

11

The Turning of the Screws—What the Lender May Demand

The promissory note that recites the terms of your mortgage loan may contain any of a number of conditions that are designed to protect the lender's interests. Assuming that you're entering into this deal in good faith, most of these conditions should cause you no particular angst. A few, however, can have implications for your legitimate plans; in any case you should be aware of what might lie in wait. Some of the more common conditions are these:

Recourse

In you're an individual investor and almost certainly if your experience is limited, the lender will probably insist on a loan "with recourse." This means that, if you default, the lender can come after your personal assets if necessary in order to recover what's owed. This is true even if you take title to the property as Albatross Investments, LLC, or some other partnership or nonpersonal entity. You can still take title in this way, but you'll need to sign the note providing your personal guarantee. If you're an experienced investor assembling a partnership of significant size, then the lender might write the loan "without recourse."

Assignment of Rents

Another form of security is the assignment of rents. With this condition, if you don't make your mortgage payments the lender reserves the right to get between you and your tenants, collect their rent directly, and apply what's necessary to bring your debt payments up to date. You might not see such a clause in a loan for a one- to four-family residence, but you can count on it as standard operating procedure for just about all commercial and larger residential property loans.

Restrictions on Secondary Financing

Increasingly typical is a provision that prevents you from obtaining any secondary financing without the primary lender's prior approval. You can probably appreciate why a lender might become uneasy if, shortly after you close the loan, you suck your equity investment back out. The property might have had sufficient income to satisfy the primary lender's required Debt Coverage Ratio with only one loan, but it might not have enough to handle a second mortgage as well. If that were the case, then there would be a real chance that someone is not going to get paid. On the other hand, if you are several years into this deal and the property is generating enough cash to cover the two loans, the primary lender might be willing to sign off on the second loan.

Lockout Period and Prepayment Penalty

As I mentioned earlier, loans that are packaged for resale as part of CMBSs (collateralized mortgage-backed securities) will usually include a lockout period of several years during which you cannot retire the loan. Both CMBS and non-CMBS loans on commercial property will often include a prepayment penalty, assessed as a percentage of the outstanding loan balance, if you pay off more than a certain amount of principal in a given year. The penalty is usually in place only during the early years of the loan (in the case of CMBS, after the lockout period). If you contemplate selling or refinancing at a time when a prepayment penalty would kick in, you need to consider whether that penalty is going to place too great a damper on your deal. At the very least you need to know when the penalty expires. Imagine how upset you would be if you sold or refinanced a property only to discover that you could have done so a short time later without a penalty.

Periodic Financial Statements

Some lenders will require that you provide an updated personal financial statement every year. As I mentioned above, it was precisely because of such a loan that I wrote, for my own use, the *Personal Financial Statement* software that my company now sells at realdata.com. Presumably the lender wants this information in order to keep its finger on your financial pulse. If the financial statement shows signs that you're becoming overextended, then the lender my decide to step in more quickly and decisively at the first sign of late or missed payments. Whether you decide to use software or a pen-and-paper form, update your in-house copy of the form whenever a significant financial event occurs—when you buy or sell a property, refinance a mortgage, pay off a loan, or open a new bank account. Then, if you need to provide a statement on short notice, it will take a minimal amount of time and effort.

12

How to Read a Closing Statement

If you have persevered through the search for a property, the due diligence, the quest for financing, and the contract negotiations, you might at last find yourself at the closing table. The pile of papers will probably dwarf the stack at the firehouse Sunday-morning pancake breakfast, and buried in there will be one that you'll want to review with care. It's called the "Closing Statement" or "Settlement Statement," and its purpose is to account for all the money—where it came from and where it went.

Depending on where you do business, the person who prepares this statement might be called the closing agent, settlement agent, escrow agent, or closing attorney. If the property is a financed one- to four-family home, the Real Estate Settlement Procedures Act (RESPA) mandates that the settlement charges and the buyer's and seller's accounts be summarized on a standard form called the "HUD-1." Although this form—shown in Figure 12.1—is not required for commercial transactions or residential properties greater than four units, it serves well as a model for understanding the flow of funds in just about any closing. I'll use it here to illustrate how the money gets sorted out.

If you sit at a closing, the settlement agent will probably begin his or her explanation by working from the back of the form to the front, so I'll do the same. Page two is where all of the settlement charges are reported. I'll break this down, as the form does, by row number in groups of hundreds.

B. Type of Loan

| 1. ☐ FHA | 2. ☐ FmHA | 5. ☐ Conv. Unins. | 6. File Number: | 7. Loan Number: | 8. Mortgage Insurance Case Number: |
| 4. ☐ VA | 5. ☐ Conv. Ins | | | | |

C. Note: This form is furnished to give you a statement of actual settlement costs. Amounts paid to and by the settlement agent are shown. Items marked "(p.o.c.)" were paid outside the closing; they are shown here for informational purposes and are not included in the totals.

D. Name & Address of Borrower:	E. Name & Address of Seller:	F. Name & Address of Lender:

G. Property Location:	H. Settlement Agent:	
	Place of Settlement:	I. Settlement Date:

J. Summary of Borrower's Transaction		K. Summary of Seller's Transaction	
100. Gross Amount Due From Borrower		**400. Gross Amount Due To Seller**	
101. Contract sales price		401. Contract sales price	
102. Personal property		402. Personal property	
103. Settlement charges to borrower (line 1400)		403.	
104.		404.	
105.		405.	
Adjustments for items paid by seller in advance		**Adjustments for items paid by seller in advance**	
106. City/town taxes to		406. City/town taxes to	
107. County taxes to		407. County taxes to	
108. Assessments to		408. Assessments to	
109.		409.	
110.		410.	
111.		411.	
112.		412.	
120. Gross Amount Due From Borrower		**420. Gross Amount Due To Seller**	
200. Amounts Paid By Or In Behalf Of Borrower		**500. Reductions In Amount Due To Seller**	
201. Deposit or earnest money		501. Excess deposit (see instructions)	
202. Principal amount of new loan(s)		502. Settlement charges to seller (line 1400)	
203. Existing loan(s) taken subject to		503. Existing loan(s) taken subject to	
204.		504. Payoff of first mortgage loan	
205.		505. Payoff of second mortgage loan	
206.		506.	
207.		507.	
208.		508.	
209.		509.	
Adjustments for items unpaid by seller		**Adjustments for items unpaid by seller**	
210. City/town taxes to		510. City/town taxes to	
211. County taxes to		511. County taxes to	
212. Assessments to		512. Assessments to	
213.		513.	
214.		514.	
215.		515.	
216.		516.	
217.		517.	
218.		518.	
219.		519.	
220. Total Paid By/For Borrower		**520. Total Reduction Amount Due Seller**	
300. Cash At Settlement From/To Borrower		**600. Cash At Settlement To/From Seller**	
301. Gross Amount due from borrower (line 120)		601. Gross amount due to seller (line 420)	
302. Less amounts paid by/for borrower (line 220)	( )	602. Less reductions in amt. due seller (line 520)	( )
303. Cash ☐ From ☐ To Borrower		**603. Cash** ☐ To ☐ From Seller	

Section 5 of the Real Estate Settlement Procedures Act (RESPA) requires the following: • HUD must develop a Special Information Booklet to help persons borrowing money to finance the purchase of residential real estate to better understand the nature and costs of real estate settlement services; • Each lender must provide the booklet to all applicants from whom it receives or for whom it prepares a written application to borrow money to finance the purchase of residential real estate; • Lenders must prepare and distribute with the Booklet a Good Faith Estimate of the settlement costs that the borrower is likely to incur in connection with the settlement. These disclosures are mandatory.

Section 4(a) of RESPA mandates that HUD develop and prescribe this standard form to be used at the time of loan settlement to provide full disclosure of all charges imposed upon the borrower and seller. These are third party disclosures that are designed to provide the borrower with pertinent information during the settlement process in order to be a better shopper.

The Public Reporting Burden for this collection of information is estimated to average one hour per response, including the time for reviewing instructions, searching existing data sources, gathering and maintaining the data needed, and completing and reviewing the collection of information.

This agency may not collect this information, and you are not required to complete this form, unless it displays a currently valid OMB control number. The information requested does not lend itself to confidentiality.

FIGURE 12.1 Settlement Statement (page 1 of 2).

L. Settlement Charges

700. Total Sales/Broker's Commission based on price $ @ % =	Paid From Borrowers Funds at Settlement	Paid From Seller's Funds at Settlement
Division of Commission (line 700) as follows:		
701. $ to		
702. $ to		
703. Commission paid at Settlement		
704.		
800. Items Payable in Connection With Loan		
801. Loan Origination Fee %		
802. Loan Discount %		
803. Appraisal Fee to		
804. Credit Report to		
805. Lender's Inspection Fee		
806. Mortgage Insurance Application Fee to		
807. Assumption Fee		
808.		
809.		
810.		
811.		
900. Items Required By Lender To Be Paid In Advance		
901. Interest from to @$ /day		
902. Mortgage Insurance Premium for months to		
903. Hazard Insurance Premium for years to		
904. years to		
905.		
1000. Reserves Deposited With Lender		
1001. Hazard insurance months @ $ per month		
1002. Mortgage insurance months @ $ per month		
1003. City property taxes months @ $ per month		
1004. County property taxes months @ $ per month		
1005. Annual assessments months @ $ per month		
1006. months @ $ per month		
1007. months @ $ per month		
1008. months @ $ per month		
1100. Title Charges		
1101. Settlement or closing fee to		
1102. Abstract or title search to		
1103. Title examination to		
1104. Title insurance binder to		
1105. Document preparation to		
1106. Notary fees to		
1107. Attorney's fees to		
(includes above items numbers:)		
1108. Title insurance to		
(includes above items numbers:)		
1109. Lender's coverage $		
1110. Owner's coverage $		
1111.		
1112.		
1113.		
1200. Government Recording and Transfer Charges		
1201. Recording fees: Deed $; Mortgage $; Releases $		
1202. City/county tax/stamps: Deed $; Mortgage $		
1203. State tax/stamps: Deed $; Mortgage $		
1204.		
1205.		
1300. Additional Settlement Charges		
1301. Survey to		
1302. Pest inspection to		
1303.		
1304.		
1305.		
1400. Total Settlement Charges (enter on lines 103, Section J and 502, Section K)		

FIGURE 12.1   Settlement Statement (page 2 of 2).

700s

This is the section that accounts for the sales commission. As with all of the settlement costs, there are columns to indicate that it comes from the buyer's funds or from the seller's funds. If payment must be made to more than one agent, lines 701 and 702 can show the breakdown. The total commission is normally reported in 703. Each section of the form has lines that are unlabeled, like 704 here, which allow the settlement agent to account for items that might not fit elsewhere in the section. For example, it is typically the seller who pays the whole sales commission, but if in this deal the parties negotiated that the buyer would pay some portion, then 704 could be used to report the buyer's share.

800s

The 800s report fees associated with the loan—which party pays, and how much. Most of these will be familiar from our earlier discussion of loan fees and again there are lines to accommodate those not named. The application fee for mortgage insurance refers not to property insurance but rather to a type of loan-related insurance that allows borrowers to exceed the usual 80 percent loan-to-value limit on owner-occupied property.

Now is an appropriate time to mention an entry that you will often see on closing statements: P.O.C., which means, "Paid Outside of Closing." For example, the lender certainly required an appraisal on the property and might have also required that fee to be paid to the appraiser directly. The cost of the appraisal will appear here, but the P.O.C. notation means that the amount is not being used in any of the calculations. In other words, the cost is not coming out of anybody's funds at the closing, but it was already paid.

900s

Although mortgage interest is normally paid in arrears, there needs to be a method by which you can start your series of regular monthly payments. Collecting odd days' interest is a way of accomplishing this. Let's say that you close on June 15 and your mortgage payments are scheduled to come due on the first of every month. You don't want to pay for a full month of interest on July 1 because, as of that date, you've had the use of the lender's money for only 15 days. One solution is for the borrower to pay interest only on a per-diem basis until the first of the next month. In this case, you would pay 15 days' interest at the June 15 closing. That would take care of your use of the lender's money until the end of the month. On July 1 you would make no payment because you've already paid for the use of the lender's money through June. Because you pay interest in arrears (i.e., you normally pay for the use of the money after you have had that use), interest begins to accrue again during July and you make your first regular payment on August 1.

An alternative method that some lenders use is to give the borrower a credit for interest at the closing and then start the payment schedule without skipping a month. If you use that method in the example above, the lender would give the borrower a *credit* for 15 days' interest at the closing. The borrower would then make her first full payment on July 1. The payment includes a full of month of interest, but the borrower received a credit at the closing for the 15 days that she really didn't have to pay, so it all works out.

There might be other items, such as the mortgage insurance premium, that need to be adjusted in the same way, and the rest of the 900s section can be used for those.

1000s

It is common, though by no means universal, that the lender might require the borrower to deposit reserves for the future payment of property taxes, liability insurance, mortgage insurance, and other assessments.

For example, let's say that taxes in this town are payable semiannually and will come due three months after the closing. The lender will actually pay this tax bill on behalf of the buyer (to be sure it gets paid). Its rule is to have enough money plus a two-month cushion on hand when the bill arrives. So, three months from the closing the lender wants to have eight months' worth of property taxes held in escrow—six to pay the bill and two for the cushion.

Let's also say that the timing of the closing is such that the borrower, who pays the mortgage loan in arrears, will make her first payment two months hence. That means the lender will collect two month's worth of tax impounds through her regular payment by the times the bill comes due. (If I lost you there, look at it again: There will be three months between the closing and the arrival of the tax bill. No payment is due at the end of the first month; there will be payments at the end of months two and three, so the lender will have collected two monthly tax impounds.) The lender needs eight months of taxes. Two will come from regular payments. Six must be deposited with the lender at the closing in order to have enough.

1100s

This section reports all the various charges associated with conveying the title. In some cases the same person might perform multiple functions and include them all in one fee. For example, one attorney or one title insurance company might charge a single amount for the title abstract and examination.

1200s

There are a variety of governmental fees that either party might have to pay. Most town or county clerks charge by the page for filing deeds, mortgages, releases, etc., on the land records. Some states charge sellers a percentage of the selling price as a conveyance tax. Many jurisdictions require documentary tax stamps.

1300s

This last section catches up what might be left. It is used for pest, radon, and structural inspections, home warranties, and just about anything else that doesn't fit elsewhere among the settlement charges. Many of these are likely to be identified as P.O.C.—paid outside of closing.

Add up all the non-P.O.C. items and you will have the total settlement charges paid from the borrower's funds at settlement and from the seller's. When the settlement agent completes these, she will bring these totals to the front page and use them in each party's transaction summary. Back now to page 1.

100s and 400s

The 100s are used to calculate the gross amount due from the borrower. The borrower has to pay the contract sales price for the real property, plus the price of any personal property, plus his or her settlement costs. In addition, the buyer might have to reimburse the seller for items the seller paid in advance but which are now the buyer's obligation. For example, if the property taxes bill arrives semiannually and the seller paid the bill two months ago, the buyer has to reimburse the seller for four months of taxes. That's because the seller already paid the next four months, but the new buyer will have possession of the property during that time and is responsible for the cost. The same sort of adjustment can be made for any obligation that might have been paid in advance, such as county taxes, sewer assessments, etc.

The bottom line, row 120, is the total that the borrower must pay, using cash and financing.

The 400s are the mirror image, resulting in the gross amount due to the seller on line 420. Note that the contract sales price, personal property, and items paid by seller in advance were all due from the buyer and the same amounts are due *to* the seller. The settlement charges that were due from the borrower (line 103) of course are not payable to the seller.

200s

Where will the money come from to pay what is due from the borrower? The buyer's cash is accounted for on line 201, and the sum of all new mortgage loans on 202. If the buyer is also assuming existing loans, they get counted on 203. If the buyer is still short of cash and is throwing in his 1964 Corvette, that can go on one of the six unlabeled lines that follow.

Just as the seller might have paid certain items in advance, there might be obligations that are related to a period of time before the closing but which also must be paid in order to convey title. "Adjustments for Items Unpaid by Seller," Rows 210 through 219 and 510 through 519, can accommodate these. Say, for example that the town sends out a sewer and water bill for past usage. The seller must give the buyer a credit equal to his usage as of the time of closing. Then, when the new buyer receives the bill, she pays it all, using the seller's money and her own.

If this is an income property, the tenants almost always pay rent in advance. That is, rent paid to the owner on April 1 is intended to cover April 1 through April 30. If the seller has collected April's rent and is conveying the property on April 16, then the seller needs to give half of that rent money to the buyer—the part that represents the property's income from the 16th through the 30th. Assuming he hasn't already done so outside the closing, this is another example of an "adjustment for items unpaid by seller."

Once the math at the bottom of the page is complete, it will be clear that there is either cash due *from* borrower or *to* the borrower. The latter can occur if the borrower gave a cash deposit that was greater than necessary to meet his or her obligations.

Keep in mind that, while the HUD-1 form is required only for closings on one- to four-family homes, the settlement agent for a commercial or larger multifamily transaction will surely provide a closing statement that summarizes similar information. The difference will be in form more than substance.

All of this will make more sense using real numbers. Consider a transaction where the property being sold is a three-family house. Here are the details:

Selling price: $250,000
Down payment: 25 percent
Amount financed: 75 percent; loan requires payment of 1 point
Closing date: April 17, 2006
Sales commission: 5 percent
Seller's existing mortgage, to be paid off: $122,311.00
Paid in advance by seller: Property taxes through June 30, 2006, $935.59
Unpaid by seller: Water and sewer up to date of closing, metered at $271.53
Prepaid rent received by seller: $1400 for the period from the closing to
    April 30
Security deposits, including interest, held by seller: $5602.11
Settlement charges to be paid by buyer (borrower):
    One loan point (as noted above)
    Credit report, $35
    Mortgage interest from 4/17 to 4/30/06 at $36.31 per day
    Title search, $300
    Document preparation, $75

Attorney's fees, $800

Title insurance policy, $1400

Recording fees, $12 for the deed, $24 for the mortgage

Tax stamps, $275

State conveyance tax. 0.5 percent of selling price

Lender's impounds of 2 months' hazard insurance at $110 per month and
6 months' taxes at $379.13 per month

Appraisal fee of $275, paid outside the closing

Settlement charges to be paid by buyer (borrower):

Sales commission of 5 percent

Recording of release of mortgage, $6

That seems like a lot of information, but the HUD-1 format will help you
to organize who pays what and to see how the settlement agent calculates
the amount due from or to each party. Figure 12.1 shows the completed
closing statement:

As I mentioned earlier, it is always easier to understand what's going on
by starting with the settlement charges on page 2. The first item is the seller's commission, 5 percent of the sales price or $12,500. That will be paid
out the seller's funds so it goes on the second column. Note that the only
other settlement charge that the seller incurs is $6 for recording the release
of the mortgage he is paying off.

The rest of the settlement charges in this example are paid the buyers,
who of course are also the borrowers. In connection with the loan (which is
75 percent of the purchase price, or $187,500) they pay one point—
$1875—and $35 for a credit report. Before the closing they paid $275 for
an appraisal. That amount is noted here but doesn't enter into the calculations because it is a "P.O.C."—paid outside of closing.

The lender will collect $544.64 interest from the day of the closing
until the end of the month. The borrowers therefore have paid (in advance,
actually) for the use of the money through April. No payment is due on May
1 because such a payment would be for use of the lender money during
April. The first payment to the bank will be on June 1.

The lender will also impound funds to have them on hand to pay future
property tax and insurance bills. Because the borrowers have just presented
a paid bill showing that they obtained insurance for the coming year, the

U.S. Department of Housing
and Urban Development

OMB Approval No. 2502-0265

B. Type of Loan

1. ☐ FHA	2. ☐ FmHA	3. ☒ Conv. Unins	6. File Number:	7. Loan Number:	8. Mortgage Insurance Case Number:
4. ☐ VA	5. ☐ Conv. Ins.		12345	67890-1	

C. Note: This form is furnished to give you a statement of actual settlement costs. Amounts paid to and by the settlement agent are shown. Items marked "(p.o.c)" were paid outside the closing; they are shown here for informational purposes and are not included in the totals.

D. Name & Address of Borrower:	E. Name & Address of Seller:	F. Name & Address of Lender:
Ebb and Flo Brooks 99 Riparian Run Torrent, CA 99999	Cosmo Politano 7 Hills St. Rubicon, CA 99999	First Foreclosure Savings & Loan 11 Sunset Ave. Torrent, CA 99999

G. Property Location:	H. Settlement Agent: Marshall, Jay & Taney	
101 Lois Lane Torrent, CA 99999 Map/Block 1986-33	Place of Settlement: 1 East Capitol St. Torrent, CA 99999	I. Settlement Date: April 17, 2006

J. Summary of Borrower's Transaction		K. Summary of Seller's Transaction	
100. Gross Amount Due From Borrower		**400. Gross Amount Due To Seller**	
101. Contract sales price	250,000.00	401. Contract sales price	250,000.00
102. Personal property		402. Personal property	
103. Settlement charges to borrower (line 1400)	9,125.42	403.	
104.		404.	
105.		405.	
Adjustments for items paid by seller in advance		*Adjustments for items paid by seller in advance*	
106. City/town taxes 04/17/06 to 06/30/06	935.59	406. City/town taxes 04/16/06 to 06/30/06	935.59
107. County taxes to		407. County taxes to	
108. Assessments to		408. Assessments to	
109.		409.	
110.		410.	
111.		411.	
112.		412.	
120. Gross Amount Due From Borrower	260,061.01	**420. Gross Amount Due To Seller**	250,935.59
200. Amounts Paid By Or In Behalf Of Borrower		**500. Reductions In Amount Due To Seller**	
201. Deposit or earnest money	62,500.00	501. Excess deposit (see instructions)	
202. Principal amount of new loan(s)	187,500.00	502. Settlement charges to seller (line 1400)	12,506.00
203. Existing loan(s) taken subject to		503. Existing loan(s) taken subject to	
204.		504. Payoff of first mortgage loan	122,311.00
205.		505. Payoff of second mortgage loan	
206.		506.	
207.		507.	
208.		508.	
209.		509.	
Adjustments for items unpaid by seller		*Adjustments for items unpaid by seller*	
210. City/town taxes to		510. City/town taxes to	
211. County taxes to		511. County taxes to	
212. Assessments to		512. Assessments to	
213. Water and sewer	271.53	513. Water and sewer	271.53
214. Prepaid rent	1,400.00	514. Prepaid rent	1,400.00
215. Security deposits plus statutory interest	5,602.11	515. Security deposits plus statutory interest	5,602.11
216.		516.	
217.		517.	
218.		518.	
219.		519.	
220. Total Paid By/For Borrower	257,273.64	**520. Total Reduction Amount Due Seller**	142,090.64
300. Cash At Settlement From/To Borrower		**600. Cash At Settlement To/From Seller**	
301. Gross Amount due from borrower (line 120)	260,061.01	601. Gross amount due to seller (line 420)	250,935.59
302. Less amounts paid by/for borrower (line 220)	(257,273.64)	602. Less reductions in amt. due seller (line 520)	(142,090.64)
303. Cash ☒ From ☐ To Borrower	2,787.37	**603. Cash ☒ To ☐ From Seller**	108,844.95

Section 5 of the Real Estate Settlement Procedures Act (RESPA) requires the following: • HUD must develop a Special Information Booklet to help persons borrowing money to finance the purchase of residential real estate to better understand the nature and costs of real estate settlement services; • Each lender must provide the booklet to all applicants from whom it receives or for whom it prepares a written application to borrow money to finance the purchase of residential real estate; • Lenders must prepare and distribute with the Booklet a Good Faith Estimate of the settlement costs that the borrower is likely to incur in connection with the settlement. These disclosures are mandatory.

Section 4(a) of RESPA mandates that HUD develop and prescribe this standard form to be used at the time of loan settlement to provide full disclosure of all charges imposed upon the borrower and seller. These are third party disclosures that are designed to provide the borrower with pertinent information during the settlement process in order to be a better shopper.

The Public Reporting Burden for this collection of information is estimated to average one hour per response, including the time for reviewing instructions, searching existing data sources, gathering and maintaining the data needed, and completing and reviewing the collection of information.

This agency may not collect this information, and you are not required to complete this form, unless it displays a currently valid OMB control number.

The information requested does not lend itself to confidentiality.

FIGURE 12.2   Settlement Statement (page 1 of 2).

162

L. Settlement Charges

700. Total Sales/Broker's Commission based on price $ 250,000 @ 5 % = $12,500.00		Paid From Borrowers Funds at Settlement	Paid From Seller's Funds at Settlement
Division of Commission (line 700) as follows:			
701. $ 12,500.00 to Fast Realty			
702. $ to			
703. Commission paid at Settlement			12,500.00
704.			
800. Items Payable In Connection With Loan			
801. Loan Origination Fee %			
802. Loan Discount 1.00 %		1,775.00	
803. Appraisal Fee 275.00 to Accurate Appraisal POC			
804. Credit Report 35.00 to First Foreclosure Savings & Loan		35.00	
805. Lender's Inspection Fee			
806. Mortgage Insurance Application Fee to			
807. Assumption Fee			
808.			
809.			
810.			
811.			
900. Items Required By Lender To Be Paid In Advance			
901. Interest from 04/17/06 to 04/30/06 @$ 36.31 /day		544.64	
902. Mortgage Insurance Premium for months to			
903. Hazard Insurance Premium for years to			
904. years to			
905.			
1000. Reserves Deposited With Lender			
1001. Hazard insurance 2 months @$ 110.00 per month		220.00	
1002. Mortgage insurance months @$ per month			
1003. City property taxes 6 months @$ 379.13 per month		2,274.78	
1004. County property taxes months @$ per month			
1005. Annual assessments months @$ per month			
1006. months @$ per month			
1007. months @$ per month			
1008. months @$ per month			
1100. Title Charges			
1101. Settlement or closing fee to			
1102. Abstract or title search to Abstract Expression		300.00	
1103. Title examination to			
1104. Title insurance binder to			
1105. Document preparation to First Foreclosure Savings & Loan		75.00	
1106. Notary fees to			
1107. Attorney's fees to Marshall, Jay & Taney		800.00	
(includes above items numbers.)			
1108. Title insurance to Tuttle Title		1,400.00	
(includes above items numbers.)			
1109. Lender's coverage $ 1,400.00			
1110. Owner's coverage $			
1111.			
1112.			
1113.			
1200. Government Recording and Transfer Charges			
1201. Recording fees: Deed $ 12.00 ; Mortgage $ 24.00 ; Releases $ 6.000		36.00	6.00
1202. City/county tax/stamps: Deed $ 275.00 ; Mortgage $		275.00	
1203. State tax/stamps: Deed $; Mortgage $			
1204. State conveyance tax		1,250.00	
1205.			
1300. Additional Settlement Charges			
1301. Survey to			
1302. Pest inspection to			
1303. Courier		40.00	
1304.			
1305.			
1400. Total Settlement Charges (enter on lines 103, Section J and 502, Section K)		9,125.42	12,506.00

Previous editions are obsolete

form HUD-1 (5/86)
ref Handbook 4305.2

FIGURE 12.2   Settlement Statement (page 2 of 2).

lender collects just two months of premiums to have as a cushion. Twelve months from now when the bill arrives, the lender will have enough to pay the bill and still have all or most of the cushion. The bank will take six months of property taxes, however. Again, it wants to keep a two-month cushion. The semiannual tax bill is due in July. By that time the borrowers will have made mortgage payments in June and July. The lender wants to have enough on hand for the six-month tax bill and the two-month cushion. If it will collect two months through the regular mortgage payments in June and July, then it needs to take six more at closing to have enough.

There are several charges related to the legal and title work, as you see listed on the form. Very often one firm will perform several of the tasks listed here and combine them into a single bill, so the use of categories here might differ from closing to closing.

You can count on your local and state governments to see your transaction as an opportunity to get a little piece of the action. There will be fees for filing documents, for tax stamps, and possibly a tax on the conveyance itself.

The final section of the form is for miscellany. Because someone is always late delivering a vital document, I've included a charge for overnight courier here.

The total of settlement charges for each party appears at the bottom. In our example, the buyers/borrowers will pay $9125.42 and the seller $12,506.00.

> ***Rule of Thumb:*** *Don't look at the total settlement charges as necessarily being what it costs you to close the transaction. The term "charges" is misleading here because the total at the bottom of the page includes the amounts that you will place in reserve with the lender for taxes and insurance. When you think of a charge you probably think of a fee paid. Putting money into a reserve account is like taking it from one pocket and putting it into another. It's still your money. You needed to put it on the table at the closing, but you haven't spent it yet.*

Now that you know the total so-called settlement charges for each party, you can bring these amounts back to the first page and resolve where the money is coming from and where it going. This page is essentially a statement of the sources and uses of funds for buyer and seller.

On the buyers' side, the uses of funds include the purchase price of the property, the settlement charges we calculated on page 2, and a reimbursement to the seller for paying property taxes in advance. That all adds up to $260,061.01. Where is it coming from? Most of it will come from the down payment ($62,500) and the mortgage loan ($187,500). The seller also has to give the buyer money in the form of a credit for three items. The seller has used metered water and sewer service worth $271.53 up to the day of the closing. He will give that amount to the buyers, and then the buyers will pay the full amount of the next water/sewer bill when it arrives. The seller has also collected a full month of rent from the tenants for April, but needs to prorate that and give the buyers an amount ($1400) that represents their share of the month's rental income. Finally, the seller is holding the tenant's security deposits, plus interest, and must turn those over to the new owners. The amount is $5602.11. The down payment, the mortgage loan, and the credits from the seller add up to $257,273.64. These are the sources of funds.

If the buyers' sources of funds (in this case down payment, mortgage loan, and credits from seller) are less than their uses of funds (purchase price, settlement costs, and credit *to* the seller), then the buyers need to bring some more cash to the closing to make up the difference. In this example, they are $2787.37 short, so that is the check they will write to complete the transaction.

The right-hand side of the page shows how the seller's account works out. He is expecting to receive the selling price of $250,000 plus reimbursement of $935.59 for his prepaid property taxes. Those are his sources of funds from this transaction. No doubt he would like to stop reading right there, but he has cash flowing in the other direction as well. He has settlement charges of $12,506 that we brought over from the second page. He also has a mortgage on the property that has to be paid off in the amount of $122,311. Finally there are those three credits he must give to the buyer for water/sewer, prepaid rent, and security deposits. All of these total $142,090.64. When the dust settles he will see his $250,935.59 reduced by this amount, leaving him with $108,844.95 cash proceeds. His one remaining hurdle will occur after the closing when he sits down with his accountant to determine how much of this amount might ultimately have to go to pay the tax on his capital gain.

Again, if your transaction is not a one- to –four-family property, your closing statement probably won't look exactly like the HUD-1 form. You might see just your side of the transaction as buyer or seller. Whatever the format, the underlying logic—a summary of settlement charges and an accounting of the sources and uses of funds—should be the same.

> ***Rule of Thumb:*** *You can and should ask to see a draft of your closing statement before you actually arrive at the closing. You might not get it, but you can ask. In this modern age of electronic processing and communication, you would think that the preparation for a closing would be completed comfortably in advance. The reality seems to be the opposite. I've sat at closings recently where I waited for payoff figures and documents to arrive via email or fax. Maybe everyone waits until the last minute because they can.*
>
> *If you're not able to see and study the closing statement early, then feel free to make everyone wait while you scrutinize it at the closing. Errors do occur, and you should not presume, just because you're signing papers on a polished oak conference table the size of a soccer field, that everything is correct.*
>
> *I can cite living proof of this. My daughter has been a participant in three closings to date, once as a buyer and twice to refinance. She didn't share your advantage of being able to study this chapter but she is proficient with figures. She found errors on the settlement statements at each of the three closings. None of the errors, as you might guess, was in her favor. The dollar amounts weren't large, but each was sufficient to pay for dinner for two at a nice restaurant.*
>
> *If you've done your due diligence all along the way, there is no reason why you should stop when the checks are finally being passed around. Bring a calculator to the closing. Verify that the numbers are correct and that they add up. If you don't know where a figure came from, ask for an explanation. It's your money. Keep an eye on it.*

13

Forms of Ownership

There are several ways in which you can hold title to real estate. While there is no universal best choice, some are clearly better than other for most investors. Let's look at the options.

Individual Ownership

You can, of course, take title to property in your personal name as an individual. This is certainly the simplest way to do so. You'll report all taxable income from the property on your personal tax return. If there are losses, the current tax law limits the amount you can claim in a given year depending upon your Adjusted Gross Income. Like some of the other forms of ownership described below, individual ownership doesn't insulate you from any personal liability in regard to the property.

Tenancy by the Entirety and Joint Tenancy

If you and your spouse have purchased a home, you probably took title as Tenants by the Entirety. In this form of ownership, which is available only if the parties are husband and wife, each party owns an undivided interest in the whole.

With Tenancy by the Entirety, neither party can act independently of the other. One potential problem is if one spouse becomes incompetent or skips off to the South Seas, then the remaining spouse might be unable to sell or

refinance the property. This form of ownership includes the right of survivorship, so upon the death of one, the other owns the entire property.

Joint Tenancy is a similar form of ownership except that the owners do
not need to be husband and wife and any owner can choose to dissolve the
Joint Tenancy by selling his or her interest. This form also includes right of
survivorship.

If you are husband and wife buying a small income property, one of
these forms of might be acceptable. However, you have no protection
against personal liability; please finish reading this chapter because you
might find a better choice.

Tenancy in Common—The General Partnership

With Tenancy in Common, the parties each own separate but unpartitioned
shares of the property. If there are two owners, each owns a 50-percent
share; he or she can sell, give away, bequeath, or even divide the interest
into smaller shares. "Unpartitioned" means that an owner can't claim an
interest in a specific part of the physical property, as in, "I own floors one,
three, and five; you can have two, four, and six."

When two or more investors combine to own property as Tenants in
Common, they will—or certainly ought to—form what is called a General
Partnership, complete with a partnership agreement. On the positive side,
when a number of people pool their assets and talents, they also increase
their buying power. The obvious problem is how to manage one property
with six Generals and no Privates? What starts off as a "we're-going-to-be-
tycoons" love-in often dissolves into acrimony and disagreement. That's
why it's essential to start off with a partnership agreement that clearly lays
out the duties, responsibilities, and limits placed on each partner. The
agreement should also lay out the conditions and procedures under which
the property can be sold and the partnership dissolved.

You should obtain a Federal Tax I.D. for the partnership and open a separate bank account for depositing rents and paying bills. Depending on the
laws of your state and the type of property you own, you might also need to
open a trust account to hold security deposits you collect from your tenants.

This type of General Partnership will file a tax return (since it has a tax
I.D.) but is considered a pass-through entity. In other words, the partnership

pays no tax itself, but passes through to each partner a pro-rata share of taxable income or loss on tax form K-1. Again, there is no protection from personal liability.

Limited Partnership

A Limited Partnership is comprised of a General Partner and some number of Limited Partners. The General Partner puts the deal together, is responsible for the management of the property, and assumes complete and unlimited liability for the activities of the partnership. The GP may receive a fee for his or her efforts. The GP may also receive a share of income or cash flow from the partnership, not necessarily (and in fact not usually) in proportion to capital invested.

The Limited Partners are so called because their exposure is limited to the amount of cash they invest, and they have no control over the running of the partnership. They sometimes receive a "preferred return" on their investment. The way this usually works is that the cash flow available for distribution each year goes first to pay the LPs a specified return on their cash. After that distribution is made—and after it gets caught up if, in a given year, there isn't enough money to satisfy the requirement—then whatever cash is left is split between the General Partner and the Limiteds. It's not uncommon for the LPs to receive most of the cash flow from the year-to-year operation of the property and for the GP to get a meaningful chunk of the proceeds from the eventual resale.

Only if you are an experienced investor or developer looking to raise capital from silent partners should you consider trying to assemble a Limited Partnership. If you're a beginner, you could invest as an LP because your activities would be confined to writing a check and signing a partnership subscription document. Chances are you're reading this book because you aspire to a more active involvement.

C Corporation

The C Corp is an independent entity; it has a life of its own. You'll need to file Articles of Incorporation with your state, select officers, appoint a board of directors, and keep minutes of an annual meeting. The C Corp will pay taxes on its income by filing form 1120.

The C Corp will do an effective job of insulating it owners from most personal liability. If a tenant chooses to sue for some grievance or injury that exceeds what you are insured for, then only your corporate assets (not your personal assets such as home or bank account) are at risk. I can hear what you're thinking and you can forget it. You will *not* escape personal responsibility for your mortgage debt if the deal goes bad, because the lender is going to require the partners' personal guarantees on any mortgage debt.

Don't misinterpret a corporation's ability to protect you from personal liability as a blank check for questionable behavior. Typically, officers and directors will be personally accountable for actions—or failures to act— that break the law. For example, in some jurisdictions if a corporate property owner fails to correct building code violations the corporate officers and directors may be held criminally liable.

There is more that one can say about the C Corp, but in regard to using it as a way to own real estate, the following rule of thumb tells you what you need to know.

> **Rule of Thumb:** *Never hold real estate in a C Corp. Sorry to equivocate like that—perhaps you can guess that there's a story here. More than 30 years ago, a very good friend and I, along with our wives, decided to form a partnership to invest in income property. I am happy to report that we are still very good friends and spouses, proving that good will can transcend bad advice. The bad advice came from the attorney who closed our first deal. He suggested we cover our assets by taking title as a C Corp. We managed the property well, created value, and embarked on a sale to realize our gain. That's when our CPA told us that we faced double taxation. When a C Corp owns and sells a property, the corporation must pay taxes on the gain. Now the remaining cash is still in the corporation. To get it out of there and into our pockets, we would have to pay it to ourselves as dividends or salary, and upon either event it would be taxed again.*
>
> *The moral of the story is unambiguous. You can achieve the benefit of protection from liability without falling victim to the double-tax whammy. Real estate and C Corps don't mix.*

Subchapter S Corporation

The Subchapter S Corporation offers the same type of protection as the C Corp. As long as you follow the formalities associated with the corporate structure—holding an annual meeting (even if you are just one person), keeping minutes, issuing stock, naming officers and directors, filing annual report with the state—you have the protection of the corporate veil for your personal assets. The primary difference is that the S Corp is a pass-through entity for tax purposes. The tax liability generated by the S Corp is passed through to the shareholders, so double taxation is not a problem.

The Sub S Corporation is limited to 75 shareholders and one class of stock. It cannot have shareholders who are not U.S. citizens.

One tax problem that you might encounter is that losses passed through to each stockholder in the Sub S Corporation are generally limited to the amount of that stockholder's investment.

Limited Liability Company

The Limited Liability Company has become the favorite vehicle of real estate investors. It provides essentially the same protection from liability as a corporation; it is a pass-through entity for tax purposes; it is simpler (read, less expensive) to set up; and it is easier to maintain because it does not require observance of corporate formalities such as annual meetings, minutes books, and the like.

Another benefit is that a one-person LLC doesn't even have to file an informational tax return but can instead report its activities on the individual's personal return.

Most states require that LLCs have a predefined termination date, generally 30 years. As a practical matter, this shouldn't be an issue. A lot can happen in 30 years, not the least likely of which is the sale of your investment property.

> *Rule of Thumb: You saw this one coming. The winner is—the LLC. It's simple and flexible and provides the same protection against liability as a corporation. It's a pass-through tax entity so there is no double-taxation. It is less expensive to set up and less burdensome to maintain than an S-Corp. No contest.*

14

The Morning After— What Do You Do Now That You're the Owner?

A good number of books have been written on the subject of property management. I won't suggest that a part of a chapter here will begin to cover this topic completely, but there are some general comments that can help you start off on the right path. Look at this final section as one big *Rule of Thumb*.

The Past Is Not Prologue

If you take over a property with tenants in place, you may find yourself in one of two situations:

1. The previous owner was a miserable cur. The tenants have festering grievances. They greet you with distrust because all you landlords are alike.

2. The previous owner was a sweetheart, a real Mother Teresa but with suspenders and a cigar. They greet you with distrust because you couldn't possibly be like him.

You should confine your concerns about this property's past to rooting out deferred maintenance of the physical property and that's about all. The management style of the previous owner is irrelevant to your operation of the property. Tenants who occupy a property when it is sold will naturally be wary of a new owner. In time all of that will pass because you won't be new anymore and, through turnover, they won't be tenants anymore. In the meantime, ignore it. Don't try to be the rent Nazi to establish that you're the boss; don't try to be just one of the guys to warm up landlord-tenant relations. Operating an investment property is a business, so conduct yourself in a professional and businesslike manner.

Golden Rules

There is something about the landlord-tenant relationship that seems to invite acrimony. Perhaps it is some detritus left over in our collective subconscious from the feudal age that turns otherwise reasonable individuals into combatants. Step outside this mindset before you begin your career as an income property owner. I am not suggesting that you should be naïve, that you should believe everything you're told or assume that every person you deal with will do the right thing. If you want to receive respect, you should start by giving it. Don't treat your tenants as if they are bad checks waiting to happen. You had enough confidence in the tenant to sign a lease with him or her. Your words and actions should convey that you expect all parties are and will act like responsible adults.

I mentioned above that you should always conduct yourself in a businesslike manner. If you follow your nose to an open container of week-old kitchen garbage, don't launch into an aria such as, "You slob; were you brought up in a pig sty?" Better is a direct comment, followed by a written missive along the lines, "We prohibit the accumulation of household trash in hallways and apartments because such trash can attract vermin. All trash must be placed regularly in the sealed containers we provide for that purpose. This rule is essential for your own safety and protection and for that of other occupants in the building. Thank you in advance for your cooperation." It's business, not personal. If you don't get the cooperation you need, you can escalate to the next level, again keeping the matter on a strictly business basis.

> ***Rule of Thumb:*** *A rule within a rule, so to speak. No matter how responsibly and professionally you conduct yourself, sooner or later you will encounter those tenants of mass destruction who make you so angry that you begin to harbor bizarre fantasies of anatomically improbable methods of revenge. Calm down. Getting angry will only make matters worse. If you own income property long enough, everything averages out. Most people you deal with will be fine; a few will drive you nuts, while some will actually exceed your hopes and expectations. Occasionally the tenants you would like to throttle become the source of instructive anecdotes, like the one you'll find below.*

There is another Golden Rule that is absolutely essential. If you expect your tenants to treat the property with respect, then you must do so as well. Maintenance and safety issues are not a place to cut corners. If something is broken, fix it. If something is dirty, clean it up. If something is dangerous, make it safe. You can be certain that very few tenants will put forward any special effort to take care of the property if your attitude is one of neglect.

Inadequate maintenance is almost always more costly than aggressive maintenance. If there is a problem, sooner or later you'll have to fix it, and then the cost will be greater as the scope of the repair enlarges over time. A poorly maintained property cannot command top rent, a fact that diminishes your cash flow and reduces the property's value at resale. I actually encourage my tenants to let me know if anything is wrong, either within their own rental unit or in any common area.

I recall an incident where a tenant was having a problem with a toilet. Instead of calling me, he put planks across the bathroom floor to act as a footbridge. The problem was nothing more than the flexible filler tube inside the toilet tank; it had come off its holder, so it sprayed water up under the lid and onto the floor. It could have been fixed in a matter of seconds. Ever since that incident, I have always told new tenants that I want to be informed of any possible maintenance issue and that I will make the judgment as to whether it merits immediate attention.

You Need a Team

You might not think that you need much of a support system, especially if you have only one or a few tenants. You may not require help on a daily basis, but you should certainly start off on day one by identifying whom you will call when you do need assistance. Depending on the type of property you own, you'll need some or all of the following:

Attorney—Perhaps the same person who handled your closing, perhaps not. The very first item you need is a lease agreement. There are standard forms you can purchase, but the one you choose might not be suitable for your kind of property or your jurisdiction. You might be able to adapt the lease format used by the previous owner. If you're considering this, you should still have the attorney review it. If the property is commercial, you should definitely have legal counsel in regard to the lease. In any legal document, what is said or left unsaid doesn't always mean what it appears to mean. Once you have an acceptable lease, type it into your word processor and edit the variable information whenever you sign up a new tenant.

On the subject of leases, I make it a practice always to sit with each new residential tenant and review the lease in detail. With this preemptive approach, you can often avoid later problems. I want to be sure the tenant understands his or her responsibilities, and mine as well. I also point out provisions of the lease that are of particular importance, such as the timely payment of rent and not using the security deposit as payment for the last months' rent. Commercial tenants will usually have their attorneys review and explain the lease. If that's the case, then you shouldn't interject any further explanation of your own.

Your attorney should also be someone who has familiarity with landlord-tenant issues. If you encounter a problem with a tenant, such as nonpayment of rent, you don't want to begin looking for a lawyer then to ask what to do. You should have one that you've already identified so that you can act quickly. Choose your lawyer at the start.

Accountant—If your taxes are simple and you've always done them yourself, it's not beyond imagining that you could continue to do so after purchasing a small income property. However, if you're forming a partnership, starting an LLC, making improvements to the property, or getting into any issues that are beyond the elementary, it's time to use an accountant.

Handyman—Yes, you know how to change a light bulb. You might even know how to fix a faucet, install a dishwasher, or build a dormer. That doesn't mean you're going to be available when it needs to be done. When the tenant calls to say there is a drip coming through the ceiling, you might be lying on the beach in Aruba, testifying before Congress, or attending your best friend's wedding. Anything you yourself can do will save you money, of course. But you should also find someone locally on whom you can call to take care of small repairs when you cannot. Search the newspaper, ask the neighbors. You might find a person who is semiretired and would be pleased to have occasional work.

Rental Agent—If you're dealing with a relatively small number of rental units, especially if they are all or mostly residential, then you will probably choose to serve as your own rental agent. It will mean advertising for tenants, showing the property, and screening applicants. Residential tenants will typically search newspaper advertisements, but prospective tenants for commercial property will be more likely to work through a broker; you should certainly consider engaging an agent to rent your commercial space.

Property Manager—The magnitude of the solution needs to be in proportion to the magnitude of the problem. If you buy the duplex across the street from your own home, you probably don't need the services of a professional property manager. When should you use a management company? These are the situations where I would suggest you seriously consider avoiding the do-it-yourself route:

1. *The property is not within easy traveling distance.* If you can't keep an eye on the property and can't get to it quickly to resolve minor problems, then you are better off paying someone else to take on that responsibility.
2. *The property has a large number of rental units.* If you purchase a 60-unit apartment building, you will need to spend a considerable amount of time dealing with routine management. If part of your plan is to give

up your previous job or career and manage your property instead, that's
fine. If not, you should farm the task out.

3. *You are not well acquainted with the property type.* If you bought an
   industrial building, for example, and don't know much about clear span
   and loading docks, leave the management to someone who does.
4. *Hands-on management doesn't suit your lifestyle.* You bought the property as an investment, but you prefer not to deal directly with tenants,
   agents, and contractors. Deal instead with one vendor, the management
   company, and let them handle the day-to-day running of the property.

Contractors—The need to make repairs occurs with any property. You'll
deal with repairs more efficiently and perhaps less expensively if you don't
wait for something to break before you choose who might fix it. The
handyman I suggested above might be your first line of defense, but if a
water heater breaks you'll probably need a plumber. Soon after you purchase your first property, ferret out recommendations and decide who
you'll call for plumbing repairs, drain line clearing, glass repairs, electri-
cal problems, and carpentry if the job exceeds the skills of your handyman.
Also line up your nonemergency services, such as lawn care, snow
removal, and gutter cleaning.

If you have prevailed to this point, you've learned something about
finding income properties to buy, doing your due diligence, analyzing the
financial information, securing financing, and getting off on the right foot
as an owner. Now it's up to you to put this collected wisdom into action—
to find, finance, and operate your profitable investment property.

Loan Tables

Monthly Mortgage Payment per $1—Mortgage Constant

Years	7.000%	7.125%	7.250%	7.375%	7.500%	7.625%	7.750%	7.875%	8.000%	8.125%
1	0.08652675	0.08658438	0.08664204	0.08669972	0.08675742	0.08681514	0.08687288	0.08693064	0.08698843	0.08704624
2	0.04477258	0.04482927	0.04488600	0.04494277	0.04499959	0.04505645	0.04511336	0.04517030	0.04522729	0.04528432
3	0.03087710	0.03093428	0.03099153	0.03104884	0.03110622	0.03116366	0.03122116	0.03127873	0.03133637	0.03139406
4	0.02394624	0.02400428	0.02406240	0.02412061	0.02417890	0.02423728	0.02429574	0.02435429	0.02441292	0.02447164
5	0.01980120	0.01986023	0.01991936	0.01997860	0.02003795	0.02009740	0.02015696	0.02021662	0.02027639	0.02033627
6	0.01704301	0.01710909	0.01716931	0.01722965	0.01729011	0.01735071	0.01741142	0.01747227	0.01753324	0.01759434
7	0.01509268	0.01515386	0.01521518	0.01527666	0.01533828	0.01540004	0.01546195	0.01552401	0.01558621	0.01564856
8	0.01363372	0.01369601	0.01375846	0.01382108	0.01388387	0.01394682	0.01400994	0.01407323	0.01413668	0.01420029
9	0.01250628	0.01256968	0.01263328	0.01269705	0.01276102	0.01282516	0.01288950	0.01295401	0.01301871	0.01308360
10	0.01161085	0.01167537	0.01174010	0.01180504	0.01187018	0.01193552	0.01200106	0.01206681	0.01213276	0.01219891
11	0.01088410	0.01094974	0.01101561	0.01108170	0.01114801	0.01121454	0.01128129	0.01134826	0.01141545	0.01148286
12	0.01028381	0.01035056	0.01041756	0.01048479	0.01055226	0.01061997	0.01068792	0.01075611	0.01082453	0.01089318
13	0.00978074	0.00984860	0.00991671	0.00998508	0.01005370	0.01012258	0.01019172	0.01026110	0.01033074	0.01040063
14	0.00935401	0.00942295	0.00949218	0.00956167	0.00963143	0.00970147	0.00977177	0.00984234	0.00991318	0.00998429
15	0.00898828	0.00905831	0.00912863	0.00919923	0.00927012	0.00934130	0.00941276	0.00948450	0.00955652	0.00962882
16	0.00867208	0.00874318	0.00881458	0.00888628	0.00895828	0.00903058	0.00910317	0.00917606	0.00924925	0.00932273
17	0.00839661	0.00846876	0.00854122	0.00861400	0.00868709	0.00876050	0.00883421	0.00890824	0.00898257	0.00905720
18	0.00815502	0.00822821	0.00830172	0.00837556	0.00844973	0.00852423	0.00859904	0.00867417	0.00874963	0.00882539
19	0.00794192	0.00801613	0.00809068	0.00816556	0.00824079	0.00831635	0.00839224	0.00846846	0.00854501	0.00862189
20	0.00775299	0.00782820	0.00790376	0.00797967	0.00805593	0.00813254	0.00820949	0.00828677	0.00836440	0.00844236
21	0.00758472	0.00766091	0.00773747	0.00781439	0.00789166	0.00796929	0.00804727	0.00812560	0.00820428	0.00828330
22	0.00743424	0.00751140	0.00758893	0.00766684	0.00774510	0.00782374	0.00790273	0.00798208	0.00806178	0.00814183
23	0.00729919	0.00737730	0.00745579	0.00753465	0.00761389	0.00769350	0.00777348	0.00785382	0.00793453	0.00801558
24	0.00717760	0.00725663	0.00733605	0.00741586	0.00749605	0.00757662	0.00765756	0.00773887	0.00782054	0.00790258
25	0.00706779	0.00714773	0.00722807	0.00730880	0.00738991	0.00747141	0.00755329	0.00763554	0.00771816	0.00780115
26	0.00696838	0.00704920	0.00713043	0.00721206	0.00729407	0.00737648	0.00745927	0.00754244	0.00762598	0.00770989
27	0.00687815	0.00695984	0.00704194	0.00712444	0.00720734	0.00729063	0.00737430	0.00745836	0.00754280	0.00762761
28	0.00679609	0.00687862	0.00696157	0.00704492	0.00712868	0.00721282	0.00729736	0.00738229	0.00746759	0.00755326
29	0.00672130	0.00680466	0.00688843	0.00697262	0.00705720	0.00714218	0.00722756	0.00731332	0.00739946	0.00748597
30	0.00665302	0.00673719	0.00682176	0.00690675	0.00699215	0.00707794	0.00716412	0.00725069	0.00733765	0.00742497

Monthly Mortgage Payment per $1—Mortgage Constant

Years	8.250%	8.375%	8.500%	8.625%	8.750%	8.875%	9.000%	9.125%	9.250%	9.375%
1	0.08710406	0.08716191	0.08721978	0.08727767	0.08733559	0.08739352	0.08745148	0.08750945	0.08756745	0.08762547
2	0.04534140	0.04539851	0.04545567	0.04551288	0.04557012	0.04562741	0.04568474	0.04574212	0.04579953	0.04585699
3	0.03145182	0.03150965	0.03156754	0.03162549	0.03168351	0.03174159	0.03179973	0.03185794	0.03191621	0.03197455
4	0.02453044	0.02458933	0.02464830	0.02470736	0.02476650	0.02482573	0.02488504	0.02494444	0.02500392	0.02506349
5	0.02039625	0.02045634	0.02051653	0.02057683	0.02063723	0.02069774	0.02075836	0.02081907	0.02087990	0.02094083
6	0.01765556	0.01771691	0.01777838	0.01783998	0.01790171	0.01796356	0.01802554	0.01808764	0.01814986	0.01821222
7	0.01571106	0.01577370	0.01583649	0.01589942	0.01596249	0.01602571	0.01608908	0.01615259	0.01621624	0.01628004
8	0.01426407	0.01432802	0.01439213	0.01445640	0.01452084	0.01458544	0.01465020	0.01471513	0.01478022	0.01484547
9	0.01314867	0.01321392	0.01327935	0.01334497	0.01341077	0.01347675	0.01354291	0.01360925	0.01367577	0.01374248
10	0.01226526	0.01233182	0.01239857	0.01246552	0.01253268	0.01260003	0.01266758	0.01273533	0.01280327	0.01287142
11	0.01155048	0.01161833	0.01168639	0.01175467	0.01182317	0.01189188	0.01196080	0.01202994	0.01209930	0.01216887
12	0.01096207	0.01103120	0.01110056	0.01117015	0.01123997	0.01131002	0.01138031	0.01145082	0.01152156	0.01159253
13	0.01047077	0.01054115	0.01061179	0.01068268	0.01075381	0.01082518	0.01089681	0.01096867	0.01104078	0.01111313
14	0.01005566	0.01012729	0.01019919	0.01027134	0.01034376	0.01041644	0.01048938	0.01056257	0.01063602	0.01070972
15	0.00970140	0.00977426	0.00984740	0.00992080	0.00999449	0.01006844	0.01014267	0.01021716	0.01029192	0.01036695
16	0.00939650	0.00947056	0.00954491	0.00961955	0.00969447	0.00976967	0.00984516	0.00992093	0.00999697	0.01007330
17	0.00913214	0.00920738	0.00928292	0.00935876	0.00943489	0.00951132	0.00958804	0.00966505	0.00974235	0.00981994
18	0.00890148	0.00897787	0.00905457	0.00913159	0.00920890	0.00928653	0.00936445	0.00944267	0.00952119	0.00960001
19	0.00869909	0.00877661	0.00885446	0.00893261	0.00901109	0.00908987	0.00916897	0.00924837	0.00932808	0.00940809
20	0.00852066	0.00859928	0.00867823	0.00875751	0.00883711	0.00891702	0.00899726	0.00907781	0.00915867	0.00923984
21	0.00836266	0.00844236	0.00852239	0.00860276	0.00868345	0.00876447	0.00884581	0.00892747	0.00900945	0.00909174
22	0.00822223	0.00830298	0.00838406	0.00846548	0.00854724	0.00862933	0.00871174	0.00879448	0.00887754	0.00896092
23	0.00809700	0.00817876	0.00826087	0.00834332	0.00842610	0.00850923	0.00859268	0.00867646	0.00876057	0.00884500
24	0.00798497	0.00806772	0.00815082	0.00823427	0.00831806	0.00840218	0.00848664	0.00857143	0.00865655	0.00874199
25	0.00788450	0.00796821	0.00805227	0.00813668	0.00822144	0.00830653	0.00839196	0.00847773	0.00856382	0.00865023
26	0.00779417	0.00787881	0.00796380	0.00804914	0.00813483	0.00822087	0.00830723	0.00839394	0.00848096	0.00856832
27	0.00771278	0.00779832	0.00788421	0.00797046	0.00805705	0.00814398	0.00823125	0.00831886	0.00840679	0.00849504
28	0.00763930	0.00772571	0.00781247	0.00789959	0.00798705	0.00807486	0.00816300	0.00825147	0.00834027	0.00842938
29	0.00757286	0.00766010	0.00774770	0.00783566	0.00792396	0.00801260	0.00810158	0.00819088	0.00828051	0.00837046
30	0.00751267	0.00760072	0.00768913	0.00777790	0.00786700	0.00795645	0.00804623	0.00813633	0.00822675	0.00831749

Monthly Mortgage Payment per $1—Mortgage Constant

Years	9.500%	9.625%	9.750%	9.875%	10.000%	10.125%	10.250%	10.375%	10.500%	10.625%
1	0.08768351	0.08774157	0.08779966	0.08785776	0.08791589	0.08797403	0.08803220	0.08809039	0.08814860	0.08820683
2	0.04591449	0.04597204	0.04602962	0.04608725	0.04614493	0.04620264	0.04626040	0.04631820	0.04637604	0.04643393
3	0.03203295	0.03209141	0.03214994	0.03220853	0.03226719	0.03232591	0.03238469	0.03244353	0.03250244	0.03256142
4	0.02512314	0.02518287	0.02524269	0.02530260	0.02536258	0.02542266	0.02548281	0.02554305	0.02560338	0.02566379
5	0.02100186	0.02106300	0.02112424	0.02118559	0.02124704	0.02130860	0.02137026	0.02143203	0.02149390	0.02155587
6	0.01827469	0.01833729	0.01840002	0.01846286	0.01852584	0.01858894	0.01865216	0.01871550	0.01877897	0.01884256
7	0.01634398	0.01640807	0.01647230	0.01653667	0.01660118	0.01666584	0.01673064	0.01679559	0.01686067	0.01692590
8	0.01491089	0.01497646	0.01504220	0.01510810	0.01517416	0.01524039	0.01530677	0.01537331	0.01544002	0.01550688
9	0.01380936	0.01387642	0.01394367	0.01401109	0.01407869	0.01414646	0.01421442	0.01428255	0.01435086	0.01441935
10	0.01293976	0.01300829	0.01307702	0.01314595	0.01321507	0.01328439	0.01335390	0.01342360	0.01349350	0.01356359
11	0.01223865	0.01230864	0.01237884	0.01244925	0.01251988	0.01259071	0.01266175	0.01273300	0.01280446	0.01287612
12	0.01166373	0.01173516	0.01180681	0.01187868	0.01195078	0.01202311	0.01209565	0.01216842	0.01224141	0.01231462
13	0.01118572	0.01125855	0.01133163	0.01140493	0.01147848	0.01155226	0.01162628	0.01170053	0.01177502	0.01184974
14	0.01078368	0.01085789	0.01093235	0.01100707	0.01108203	0.01115724	0.01123269	0.01130839	0.01138434	0.01146053
15	0.01044225	0.01051781	0.01059363	0.01066971	0.01074605	0.01082265	0.01089951	0.01097662	0.01105399	0.01113161
16	0.01014990	0.01022677	0.01030392	0.01038133	0.01045902	0.01053697	0.01061519	0.01069368	0.01077242	0.01085143
17	0.00989781	0.00997596	0.01005440	0.01013311	0.01021210	0.01029137	0.01037091	0.01045073	0.01053081	0.01061116
18	0.00967911	0.00975851	0.00983820	0.00991818	0.00999844	0.01007898	0.01015980	0.01024090	0.01032228	0.01040393
19	0.00948840	0.00956900	0.00964991	0.00973110	0.00981259	0.00989436	0.00997642	0.01005877	0.01014139	0.01022429
20	0.00932131	0.00940309	0.00948517	0.00956754	0.00965022	0.00973318	0.00981643	0.00989997	0.00998380	0.01006790
21	0.00917434	0.00925725	0.00934047	0.00942398	0.00950780	0.00959191	0.00967631	0.00976101	0.00984599	0.00993125
22	0.00904461	0.00912862	0.00921293	0.00929754	0.00938246	0.00946767	0.00955318	0.00963898	0.00972507	0.00981144
23	0.00892974	0.00901480	0.00910017	0.00918584	0.00927182	0.00935809	0.00944466	0.00953152	0.00961867	0.00970611
24	0.00882775	0.00891382	0.00900020	0.00908689	0.00917389	0.00926118	0.00934877	0.00943664	0.00952481	0.00961326
25	0.00873697	0.00882402	0.00891137	0.00899904	0.00908701	0.00917527	0.00926383	0.00935268	0.00944182	0.00953123
26	0.00865599	0.00874397	0.00883227	0.00892087	0.00900977	0.00909897	0.00918846	0.00927823	0.00936829	0.00945863
27	0.00858361	0.00867250	0.00876169	0.00885118	0.00894098	0.00903106	0.00912144	0.00921210	0.00930304	0.00939425
28	0.00851882	0.00860856	0.00869861	0.00878896	0.00887960	0.00897054	0.00906176	0.00915326	0.00924504	0.00933708
29	0.00846071	0.00855128	0.00864215	0.00873331	0.00882477	0.00891651	0.00900854	0.00910084	0.00919341	0.00928624
30	0.00840854	0.00849989	0.00859154	0.00868349	0.00877572	0.00886823	0.00896101	0.00905407	0.00914739	0.00924098

Monthly Mortgage Payment per $1—Mortgage Constant

Years	10.750%	10.875%	11.000%	11.125%	11.250%	11.375%	11.500%	11.625%	11.750%	11.875%
1	0.08826509	0.08832336	0.08838166	0.08843998	0.08849831	0.08855667	0.08861505	0.08867346	0.08873188	0.08879032
2	0.04649185	0.04654983	0.04660784	0.04666589	0.04672399	0.04678213	0.04684032	0.04689854	0.04695681	0.04701512
3	0.03262045	0.03267955	0.03273872	0.03279794	0.03285723	0.03291659	0.03297601	0.03303549	0.03309503	0.03315464
4	0.02572428	0.02578486	0.02584552	0.02590627	0.02596710	0.02602801	0.02608901	0.02615009	0.02621125	0.02627250
5	0.02161795	0.02168014	0.02174242	0.02180481	0.02186731	0.02192991	0.02199261	0.02205541	0.02211832	0.02218133
6	0.01890628	0.01897012	0.01903408	0.01909816	0.01916237	0.01922670	0.01929116	0.01935573	0.01942043	0.01948525
7	0.01699127	0.01705678	0.01712244	0.01718823	0.01725417	0.01732024	0.01738646	0.01745282	0.01751932	0.01758595
8	0.01557390	0.01564108	0.01570843	0.01577593	0.01584358	0.01591140	0.01597937	0.01604751	0.01611579	0.01618424
9	0.01448801	0.01455685	0.01462586	0.01469505	0.01476441	0.01483395	0.01490366	0.01497354	0.01504360	0.01511383
10	0.01363887	0.01370434	0.01377500	0.01384585	0.01391689	0.01398813	0.01405954	0.01413115	0.01420295	0.01427493
11	0.01294799	0.01302007	0.01309235	0.01316483	0.01323752	0.01331041	0.01338350	0.01345680	0.01353029	0.01360399
12	0.01238804	0.01246169	0.01253555	0.01260963	0.01268393	0.01275844	0.01283317	0.01290810	0.01298326	0.01305862
13	0.01192469	0.01199987	0.01207527	0.01215091	0.01222677	0.01230286	0.01237918	0.01245572	0.01253248	0.01260946
14	0.01153696	0.01161363	0.01169054	0.01176769	0.01184508	0.01192270	0.01200055	0.01207864	0.01215696	0.01223551
15	0.01120948	0.01128760	0.01136597	0.01144459	0.01152345	0.01160255	0.01168190	0.01176149	0.01184131	0.01192138
16	0.01093070	0.01101022	0.01109000	0.01117004	0.01125033	0.01133086	0.01141165	0.01149268	0.01157396	0.01165549
17	0.01069178	0.01077266	0.01085381	0.01093521	0.01101687	0.01109879	0.01118096	0.01126339	0.01134606	0.01142899
18	0.01048585	0.01056804	0.01065050	0.01073322	0.01081620	0.01089945	0.01098295	0.01106671	0.01115073	0.01123499
19	0.01030747	0.01039092	0.01047464	0.01055863	0.01064288	0.01072740	0.01081218	0.01089722	0.01098251	0.01106806
20	0.01015229	0.01023695	0.01032188	0.01040709	0.01049256	0.01057830	0.01066430	0.01075056	0.01083707	0.01092384
21	0.01001679	0.01010261	0.01018871	0.01027508	0.01036171	0.01044861	0.01053578	0.01062320	0.01071088	0.01079881
22	0.00989810	0.00998503	0.01007223	0.01015971	0.01024746	0.01033547	0.01042374	0.01051227	0.01060106	0.01069010
23	0.00979382	0.00988181	0.00997008	0.01005862	0.01014742	0.01023649	0.01032581	0.01041540	0.01050523	0.01059532
24	0.00970199	0.00979099	0.00988027	0.00996981	0.01005962	0.01014969	0.01024002	0.01033060	0.01042142	0.01051250
25	0.00962093	0.00971089	0.00980113	0.00989163	0.00998240	0.01007342	0.01016469	0.01025621	0.01034798	0.01043999
26	0.00954924	0.00964012	0.00973127	0.00982268	0.00991435	0.01000627	0.01009844	0.01019085	0.01028351	0.01037640
27	0.00948574	0.00957749	0.00966950	0.00976177	0.00985429	0.00994706	0.01004008	0.01013333	0.01022682	0.01032054
28	0.00942940	0.00952197	0.00961480	0.00970788	0.00980121	0.00989478	0.00998859	0.01008264	0.01017691	0.01027141
29	0.00937934	0.00947269	0.00956629	0.00966014	0.00975423	0.00984856	0.00994312	0.01003791	0.01013292	0.01022815
30	0.00933481	0.00942890	0.00952323	0.00961781	0.00971261	0.00980765	0.00990291	0.00999840	0.01009410	0.01019001

Glossary

Abatement—In a lease, the reduction or elimination of rent for a period of time. For example, as an inducement to a tenant to rent a particular space, the landlord might abate the rent for a period of months while the tenant remodels the space.

Accelerated Depreciation—Depreciation methods that allow a taxpayer to take faster write-offs than with straight-line during the early part of an asset's useful life.

Accumulated Depreciation—The sum of annual depreciation deductions taken to date. Also, accrued depreciation.

Adjustable Rate Mortgage (ARM)—A mortgage loan in which the interest rate is not constant over the life of the loan, but is adjusted periodically according to a predetermined formula or index.

Adjusted Basis—The original cost of an asset, such as real estate, plus capital improvements, less accumulated depreciation and costs of sale. The taxable gain at the time of sale is, in general, the selling price less the adjusted basis.

Adjusted Gross Income (AGI)—Gross income less certain adjustments, including IRA, alimony, and Keogh deductions. Used to determine the investor's passive loss allowance, which under the tax code at this writing begins to phase out when the investor's AGI reaches $100,000 and is completely eliminated at $150,000.

Alternative Minimum Tax (AMT)—A tax that may be triggered if certain tax benefits, such as passive losses and accelerated depreciation, reduce an individual's income tax liability. You must use Federal tax form 6251 to determine if you are subject to the Alternative Minimum Tax.

Amortization—a) The process through which a loan is retired over time through periodic repayment of the principal. b) The process of taking a partial annual tax deduction for an item that cannot be expensed in a single year. For example, points paid to secure a loan on investment property must typically be deducted (amortized) over the life of that loan.

Annual Debt Service (ADS)—The total of all payments on a mortgage loan, including both interest and principal, for a year.

Annual Percentage Rate (APR)—A rate whose purpose is to express the true cost of a loan. The calculation of APR usually involves not only the contract interest rate of the loan, but also loan points and often various fees such as underwriting and document preparation.

Annual Property Operating Data (APOD)—A form that lists a property's gross income, individual operating expenses, and net operating income. An APOD is similar to a business profit-and-loss statement.

Appreciation—The increase over time in the value of an asset due to economic factors rather than to improvements or additions, or enhancement of the revenue stream.

Assessor—The county or municipal person or office responsible for estimating the value of real and personal property for the purpose of levying local tax. This office usually maintains certain information about each property (lot size, improvements, square footage, amenities) that are available as public records.

Assumed Mortgage—A mortgage in which the purchaser of a property assumes liability for payment of an existing mortgage loan. Typically the purchaser takes over the existing balance, terms, and payment schedule. Many mortgage loans contain a "due on sale" clause that prohibits assumption by requiring the original borrower to pay off the loan if he or she transfers title of the mortgaged property to a third party.

Balloon—A provision in a loan that requires the principal balance to be paid off in a lump sum before the loan would be retired through normal amortization. For example, a loan might be written with a 15-year amortization and a 7-year balloon. The periodic payment amount and the interest and principal portion of each payment are all calculated as if the loan were to run for 15 years. However, the borrower must retire the loan at the end of seven years by paying the balance outstanding (the balloon) at that time. Also, Balloon Payment.

Basis—The starting point for computing gain or loss on an investment; typically, the original purchase price. See also, Adjusted Basis.

Book Value—An asset's original basis less accumulated depreciation.

BOY—An acronym that means "Beginning of Year." BOY1 indicates, "Beginning of Year 1."

Capital Addition—An addition to a piece of real estate having a useful life of more than one year, or an improvement that is likely to prolong the life of the property. A capital addition is different from a repair, which maintains rather than increases the life of a property.

Capital Gain—Gain from the sale or disposition of a capital asset, such as real estate. May be long term or short term.

Capital Improvement—See Capital Addition.

Capitalization Rate—The ratio between a property's net operating income and purchase price or value. It is a measure of return before consideration of taxes, financing, or recovery of capital. If a property has a given NOI, then the higher the capitalization rate demanded by an investor, the lower the value of the property. Also called "cap rate."

Cash Flow after Taxes (CFAT)—The cash flow before taxes, reduced by the tax liability that the property generates for the owner, or increased by the tax savings.

Cash Flow before Taxes (CFBT)—During a given period, all of a property's cash inflows less all of its cash outflows. Inflows are counted whether or not they must be included as taxable income, and outflows are counted regardless of deductibility. For example, cash flow is affected by the entire amount of a mortgage payment, even though only the interest portion is deductible. Cash flow is not affected by a depreciation deduction, which is not a cash item. "Cash flow before taxes" ignores the property's effects on the owner's income tax liability.

Cash-on-Cash Return—The rate of return on an investment measured as the ratio between the cash flow before taxes and the initial cash investment.

Closing—The completion of a real estate transaction, where loan and/or deed documents are signed, and, if necessary, funds are exchanged and title is conveyed from seller to buyer

Closing Costs—Fees paid, typically to an attorney, title company, lender, and others, for documentation, representation, loan-related costs, and other related items in connection with the purchase or sale of a piece of real estate.

Commercial property—See Nonresidential Property

Commission—A fee paid, typically to a real estate agent or broker, for negotiating a loan, lease, or sale.

Common Area Maintenance (CAM) Charge—An amount of additional rent charged to a tenant for maintenance of common areas such as hallways, public restrooms, parking lots, etc. May also include a share of property taxes and insurance.

Comparable Sales Approach—A method of real estate appraisal that compares the subject property to recent sales of similar properties and adjusts for differences between the subject and the comparables.

Comparables—For purposes of valuation, properties that are similar to the subject property and that have been recently sold or leased.

Consumer Price Index (CPI)—An index published by the U.S. Bureau of Labor Statistics and widely used as a measure of inflation. The index estimates the cost of buying a fixed group of goods and services and compares that cost to the base year (1982) that was assigned an index value of 100. The CPI is commonly used in escalation clauses of commercial real estate leases so that the rent generated by those leases will keep pace with inflation. Also, cost-of-living index.

Constant Maturity Treasury Index (CMT)—An adjustable-rate mortgage index usually based on the weekly or monthly yields for one-year Treasury bills.

Cost Approach—A method of real estate appraisal that takes the cost to build the physical structure today, depreciates it to account for its age, and adds in the value of the land.

Cost of Funds Index (COFI)—An adjustable-rate mortgage index based on the rates paid on checking and savings accounts by members of the 11th district of the Federal Home Loan Bank.

Costs of Sale—Fees typically paid to a broker and/or attorney to effect the sale of a piece of real estate. These costs are not tax deductions as such. Rather, they are an adjustment to the basis of the property and thus affect the taxable gain on sale.

Debt Coverage Ratio—The ratio between an income-property's annual net operating income and its annual debt service. Most lenders require a debt coverage ratio of at least 1.2. A property with a 1.2 debt coverage ratio has income before debt service that is 1.2 times as much as the debt service—in other words, the property generates 20 percent more net income than it needs to make its mortgage payments.

Debt Service—The total loan payment, including both interest and principal.

Depreciation—Often used interchangeably with "Depreciation Allowance." Appraisers, however, typically use the term "depreciation" to represent the actual loss in value due to physical wear and tear and to functional and economic obsolescence.

Depreciation Allowance—The amount of the tax deduction that a property owner may take each year until he or she has written off the entire depreciable asset. In real estate, the physical structures are considered depreciable assets, but the land is not. Therefore, there is no depreciation allowance for the value of the land. See also Useful Life.

Discount Rate—The compound interest rate used to reduce expected future cash flows to their estimated present value.

Discounted Cash Flow Analysis (DCF)—An income-property appraisal technique that estimates value by discounting all expected future cash flows to the present and summing the discounted amounts.

Due Diligence—The process of thoroughly investigating, verifying, and analyzing all pertinent information, representations, and projections about a prospective investment.

Due on Sale Clause—A provision common to many mortgage notes that requires the borrower to pay the note in full if title to the property is transferred.

Effective Gross Income (EGI)—See Gross Operating Income.

EOY—An acronym that means "End of Year." EOY1 indicates, "End of Year 1."

Equity—The difference between a property's value and the balance of the debt against it. A property worth $1,000,000 with loans totaling $750,000 has equity of $250,000.

Estoppel Certificate—A document in which a tenant acknowledges key information about its lease terms, start and termination dates, modification and options, as well as the status of rent payments and of the presence of any defaults by the landlord.

Expense Stop—A provision in a lease where the tenant agrees to pay the excess of certain operating expenses over a base amount. The landlord pays the expense up to the amount of the expense stop, and the tenant pays or reimburses the landlord for the rest.

Fair Market Value—The price at which a property would change hands from a willing seller to a willing buyer, where neither party is under a compulsion to sell or buy and where both have reasonable knowledge of all pertinent facts. Also, Market Value.

First Mortgage—The first, or senior claim against an asset, as security for repayment of a debt.

FICO Score—A credit-rating score used by most lenders. A standard credit report on an individual will return three FICO scores, one from each of the three credit bureaus.

FSBO—For Sale by Owner; pronounced "Fizzbo."

Funded Reserves—A sum of money put aside so that it will be available to handle an extraordinary expense or improvement. For example, an investor might anticipate the need for a new roof five years after acquisition of a property and place money into a reserve account in advance so that funds are available when needed.

General Partner (GP)—The person or entity in a limited partnership that bears unlimited liability and all of the management responsibility of that partnership.

Graduated Payment Mortgage—A type of mortgage loan in which the payment gradually increases over time. Typically the early payment level(s) are insufficient to cover the interest and therefore negative amortization occurs. Eventually the payment rises to a point where the mortgage will amortize during the stated term of the loan.

Gross Operating Income (GOI)—A property's annual Gross Scheduled Income, less allowances for vacancy and credit loss. Also, Effective Gross Income.

Gross Rent Multiplier (GRM)—A method of estimating or expressing a property's value as a multiple of its gross rental income.

Gross Scheduled Income—The annual income of a property if all rentable space were in fact rented and all rent collected; the total potential income.

Half-Month Convention—A provision of the tax code as of this writing that allows only one-half month of depreciation in the month a property is acquired and one-half month in the month it is sold.

HUD-1—A form mandated by the Real Estate Settlement Procedures Act (RESPA) to summarize settlement costs in financed sales of one- to four-family homes.

Improvement—See Capital Addition.

Income Approach—A method of real estate appraisal that takes a property's project income stream and capitalizes it to estimate the value of the asset.

Income Property—Real property leased to tenants and held for the purpose of generating ongoing rental income.

Inflation—The loss of a currency's purchasing power over time.

Inflation Rate—The annual rate at which a currency loses purchasing power.

Initial Investment—The amount of cash invested at the time a property is purchased.

Interest-Only Mortgage—A mortgage loan in which the borrower makes periodic payments of interest only and pays the full principal balance at the end of the loan term.

Internal Rate of Return (IRR)—The rate of return that discounts all anticipated future net cash flows (including the reversion) back to a present value that equals the initial investment.

Lease—An agreement granting possession of land or a specified part of a building for a specified time in exchange for rent.

Lessor—An owner who leases property to a tenant; landlord.

Lessee—A tenant who leases property from a landlord.

Leverage—An investor's use of borrowed money to increase buying power.

Limited Liability Company (LLC)—A type of business entity that is taxed like a partnership (i.e., pass-through taxation) but that also provides the limited liability protection of a corporation.

Limited Partner (LP)—An investor in a limited partnership who typically has none of the management responsibility and whose liability is limited to the amount of his or her investment.

Limited Partnership—A partnership having a General Partner who manages the partnership's investments and bears unlimited liability and Limited Partners who have no management control and whose liability typically is limited to the amount of their investment.

London Interbank Offering Rate Index (LIBOR)—An adjustable-rate market-based mortgage index based on the rate London banks charge each other for interbank borrowing.

Long-Term Capital Gain—The gain on an asset held more than 12 months.

Marginal Tax Bracket—The rate at which the investor's next dollar of income will be taxed.

Market Value—See Fair Market Value.

Mortgage—A lien against a property that secures a mortgage loan or note.

Mortgagee—The lender in a mortgage agreement.

Mortgagor—The borrower in a mortgage agreement.

Net Operating Income (NOI)—A property's Gross Operating Income less the sum of all operating expenses. NOI represents a property's profitability before consideration of taxes, financing, or recovery of capital.

Net Present Value (NPV)—The discounted value of all of a property's future cash flows (including the reversion) less the initial cash investment.

Non-Residential Property—Real property that does not satisfy the definition of Residential Property; property not primarily intended for use as dwellings.

Operating Expense—Expense necessary for the maintenance of a piece of real property and to ensure its continued ability to produce income. Loan payments, depreciation, and capital expenditures are not considered operating expenses.

Owner-Occupant—A property owner who occupies part or all of his or her property.

Pass Through—An operating expense that is passed on, in whole or in part, to a tenant. For example, a lease may require that a particular tenant pay a pro-rata share of property taxes in excess of $10,000. If the tax bill is $50,000, and the tenant occupies 5 percent of the property's rentable area, then the tenant must pay 5 percent of $40,000 (the amount of the tax bill over $10,000), or $2,000. The landlord treats this as an income item; often call a "recoverable expense."

Passive Activity—A business or rental activity that the taxpayer does not materially participate in managing or running. See also, Passive Loss Allowance.

Passive Loss Allowance—The dollar amount of losses from passive-activity investments that an individual taxpayer may deduct against ordinary income. In general, losses from passive activities can only be used to offset income from other passive activities. As of this writing, an exception exists for owners of rental real estate, who may deduct up to $25,000 of net losses from rental real estate investments in which they actively participate. This allowance is reduced for taxpayers with Adjusted Gross Income over $100,000.

Periodic Interest Rate—The rate of interest per payment period. If a loan has an annual rate of 12 percent but is payable monthly, then the periodic (i.e., monthly) interest is 1 percent.

Personal Property—Property that is not permanently attached to the real estate. Appliances are personal property.

Phase I Environmental Survey—An inspection for hazards such as asbestos, PCBs, radon, underground storage tanks, lead-based paint, and contamination from waste sites; routinely required by commercial lenders.

Point(s)—A fee paid to a lender as prepaid interest or for the lender's service in making the loan. Typically a point is equal to one percent of the amount of the loan. Points are not deductible as an expense, but must be written off over the life of the loan. Also called Discount Points.

Preferred Return—In a limited partnership, a limited partner may be entitled to an annual, noncompounded return on his or her investment before the general partner receives any return.

Prepayment Penalty—A provision that is sometimes included in a mortgage note imposing a penalty if the loan is paid off substantially or in full before a certain date. The penalty is usually a percentage of the outstanding loan balance.

Present Value (PV)—The discounted value of a series of future cash flows.

Principal—The amount of a loan, exclusive of any interest.

Pro Forma—A statement or report of projections about the possible future performance of an income property. A pro forma uses assumptions as to future revenues, expenses, interest rates, tax considerations, etc.

Purchase Money Mortgage—A mortgage loan provided by the seller for all or part of a property's purchase price.

Rest Estate Settlement Procedure Act (RESPA)—A law requiring lenders to disclose settlement costs and lending practices to buyers of one- to four-family homes.

Recoverable Expense—See Pass Through.

Refinance—The process of retiring all existing loans against a property and replacing them with a new loan. In a cash-out refinance, the new loan is greater than the sum of the loans being retired, and the borrower receives the difference in cash.

Rentable Square Feet—The portion of a rental property that may be leased to tenants. For example, in a multitenant office building, the office suites themselves contain rentable space, but hallways and stairways outside those suites typically are not included as part of the rentable area.

Resale—See Reversion.

Residential Property—Real estate designed and intended as dwellings, including single- and multifamily homes, but not hotels or motels. A property that combines both residential and nonresidential uses must derive at least 80 percent of its gross rental income from dwelling units to be considered residential for purposes of depreciation. If a mixed-use property is owner-occupied, then the fair-market rental value of the owner's unit must be taken into account when determining the residential or nonresidential status of the property.

Reversion—The value of an investment at the time of its resale.

Sensitivity Analysis—An analysis where one or more independent variables is altered to determine the effect on a particular dependent variable. For example, one might test how different rental rates affect the cash flow before taxes, or how different purchase prices affect the internal rate of return.

Short-Term Capital Gain—The gain on an asset held 12 months or less.

Straight-Line Depreciation—A depreciation method that allows the owner to write off an asset's basis in equal amounts over its useful life. For example, if an asset were to have a 10-year useful life, the straight-line depreciation allowance each year would be 10 percent of the basis. Note that in the tax code as of this writing there exists a so-called half-month convention for real estate, where the taxpayer is allowed only one-half month depreciation in the month placed in service and one-half month in the month of resale.

Tax Shelter—An investment vehicle that can shield a part of an investor's ordinary income from taxation.

Tax-Deferred Exchange—A provision of the tax code (sec. 1031) that permits property owners to exchange like-kind properties. If certain criteria are met, the parties can defer recognition of gain or loss and therefore also defer the tax that might have occurred in an outright sale.

Tenant Improvements (TI)—Improvements made to a rental unit by a landlord for the benefit of a tenant. Such improvements are capital expenditures, not repairs.

Term—The number of periodic payments over which a loan is amortized.

Treasury Bill—A government obligation representing a virtually risk-free investment.

Useful Life—The length of time, as specified in the tax code, over which an asset may be depreciated. The Useful Life for tax purposes is not necessarily the same as the actual physical life expectancy of a particular asset.

Vacancy and Credit Allowance—A deduction from the Gross Scheduled Income for losses due to unoccupied space and uncollected rent.

Wraparound—A secondary mortgage loan that includes both the principal balance of the existing first loan, which remains in force, plus additional financing advanced by the wraparound lender (usually the seller of the property). The borrower makes payments on the larger secondary loan to the wraparound lender; that lender then uses a portion of the money received to continue making the payments to the primary lender.

Index

NOTE: Boldface numbers indicate illustrations or tables.

About the Author

Frank Gallinelli is founder and president of RealData® Inc., one of the top software companies serving individual real estate investors. He is the author of *What Every Real Estate Investor Needs to Know About Cash Flow.*